A PILGRIM'S PATH

Also by John J. Robinson:

BORN IN BLOOD
The Lost Secrets of Freemasonry

DUNGEON, FIRE AND SWORD
The Knights Templar in the Crusades

A PILGRIM'S PATH

One Man's Road to the Masonic Temple

JOHN J. ROBINSON

M. Evans and Company, Inc.
New York

M. Evans and Company, Inc.
216 East 49th Street
New York, New York 10017

Library of Congress Cataloging-in-Publication Data

Robinson, John J.
    A Pilgrim's path : one man's road to the Masonic Temple / John J. Robinson.
        p. cm.
    ISBN 0-87131-732-X : $17.95. – ISBN 0-87131-722-2 (pbk.) : $11.95
        1. Freemasonry – United States – History.   2. Freemasons – United States – History.   I. Title.
    HS517.R6 1993
    366'.1'0973 – dc20   93-9178
                                                                 CIP

Typeset by AeroType, Inc.

Manufactured in the United States of America

9 8 7 6 5 4 3 2 1

This book is dedicated to
the next man to become an
Entered Apprentice
through all the centuries to come.

CONTENTS

Preface

I N TALKING WITH Masonic groups across the country, I have
repeatedly been asked when I was going to write another book
about Masonry, something I had no plans to do. I have thought of
myself as a writer of history, not of Freemasonry.

More recently, I began asking Masons what they'd like to see in
such a book. The replies were numerous and varied. Many wanted to
know about fundamentalist anti-Masons: Why do they hate Freemasonry? What are their allegations against Masonry, and how
should a Mason respond? Others wanted to know about Masonry and
the public. What do non-Masons ask when they call in to radio and
TV shows about the fraternity? Had I formed any opinions regarding
the decline in Masonic membership? Does the public really care
about Masonry?

As I reflected on these and many other questions, I realized that
during my travels to talk about my books and about Masonry, I had
gained a great deal of experience, and some insight, into the questions, the problems, and the misunderstandings about Freemasonry
that do exist, both within the fraternity and outside it. Good sense
dictates that all that experience will be wasted if I don't find a way to
share it. I can only hope that this little book will provide some of the

answers, offer some solutions to problems as I understand them, and perhaps provide a few things for Masons to think about.

For non-Masons who choose to read it, this book may provide new perspectives on the world's oldest and largest fraternal society.

I am often asked a question along the lines of, "Exactly what *is* your area of expertise?" My usual answer is, "I am generally regarded as the world's foremost authority on my own personal opinions – and on nothing else."

I can't add anything to that answer, so please bear in mind that if in this book I reach a conclusion, make a judgment, or even go so far as to offer a suggestion, it doesn't come from a deep well of infallible wisdom. Everything that follows is just one man's personal opinion, based on one man's personal experiences in the world of Masonry.

1

Getting to Know You

I'VE BEEN ENGAGED in Masonic research for ten years now, but I still think of myself as a student. And I have learned what every student learns: Every time we open a door, we find a dozen more doors.

It has been stated that Freemasonry has been the subject of over fifty thousand written works since it revealed its existence to the people of London in 1717. A dedicated researcher might devote himself to learning all that there is to know about Freemasonry by reading a Masonic book every single day. The problem is that such a program would require 137 years to complete, with a few thousand more Masonic works turned out in the meantime. It can't be done.

It should always be borne in mind that precious little was actually recorded about ancient, traditional Masonry before 1717, which is hardly surprising for a group sworn to put nothing in writing. That has left a clear field for speculation and imagination, which have often been applied to elaborate on and convolute some simple, beautiful teachings of brotherhood and charity. That's not new.

Books of theology far outnumber books about Masonry, as for almost two thousand years some men have felt compelled to explain to the rest of us what Jesus Christ *really* meant in the Sermon on the

Mount, or the hidden meanings in the golden rule. It is difficult to imagine Christ talking to a crowd and then walking off down the road, leaving behind four disciples to reveal to the audience the esoteric message concealed in the parable of the Good Samaritan.

To me, the message of Freemasonry seems bright and clear, and I like what I see. It is always possible, and even probable, that my understanding is constricted by limited knowledge, and especially by the absence of the emotional involvement I would have were I a Freemason. What I do have is some observations, opinions, and experiences I would like to share, in order to pass on what I have learned from the unique experience of talking with non-Masons all across the country. I've talked with sons, daughters, and wives of Freemasons, with grateful beneficiaries of Masonic charities, and with inquisitive minds who have no Masonic connections whatever, but would like to know more. I've also talked with rabid fundamentalist anti-Masons who see Masonry as a separate, satanic cult. I've even been publicly branded a messenger of Satan for speaking favorably of the Masonic order. Some of the light I have acquired certainly has its dark side, but it has been an extraordinary experience.

I have also had the opportunity to discuss Freemasonry with Masons representing a wide variety of Masonic bodies, including Grand Lodges, Scottish Rite, York Rite, the Allied Masonic degrees, the Shrine, and others across this country and in Europe.

The research that resulted in my writing the book *Born in Blood* began with no thought of Freemasonry. I was looking at events in the history of fourteenth-century Britain, but kept bumping into things that seemed to relate to the little I knew about this ancient society. I decided to take a break from classic medieval history to learn more about Masonry.

I was overwhelmed by the amount of written material available. The local public library had hundreds of volumes on Masonry. My first book on Masonic ritual, a little volume called *Duncan's Ritual,* was purchased at my local supermarket. Others were available at a fraternal supply house run by a father and son who were both active Freemasons. Perhaps that's why I was surprised when I was later attacked for writing an "exposé" of Masonic secrets, since I mostly used works that I had purchased from Freemasons.

Nor could all of the available books of Masonic ritual be called clandestine. I found several "official" works written in simple, easy to decipher codes of abbreviations, or with graphic symbols such as a sword for the Tyler and a chair for the Worshipful Master of the lodge. One little book in cryptic symbols bore the title *Rambling Affluent Moutons and Merry Midshipmen.* The initial letters of those words meant that it was intended for Royal Arch Masons and Mark Masters. It was officially sanctioned by the "GC RAM of the Dark and Bloody Ground," which meant that it had the approval of the Grand Chapter of Royal Arch Masons of Kentucky.

The decision to spend years researching and writing a book is not an easy one. Many of us want to, but we know that it requires more than just a tremendous amount of work. Even if the book is completed, there is only a slim chance of finding a publisher. About half a million books are submitted to publishers each year in this country, and only about fifty thousand of them find their way into print. So as you write, week after week, you know that chances are ten to one that what you're struggling over will never be published. There's also the knowledge that the average book sells fewer than five thousand copies, a meager return for what may represent years of effort.

In my case, I was writing in the hope of finding something constructive to do in retirement. I had watched my father, from sixty-five to eighty-four, filling his hours making model ships, until his eyesight was not up to the fine detail and he ran out of family and friends to give them to. My writing experience had consisted of millions of words appearing in the form of advertising copy, direct mail, press releases, and corporate business reports. Most important, perhaps, I was eager to write a book because I felt that during my research into Masonic origins I had discovered something exciting, even exhilarating, that I wanted to share. It appeared that Freemasonry may well have pioneered the very concept of religious freedom, the individual right to worship God according to one's own conscience. That was a purpose far more important than the original purposes which Freemasons usually ascribed to themselves. That concept of Masonic purpose was new, and different, and important.

The excitement of being published was soon submerged in the depression of a poor reception. The introduction of *Born in Blood* was dismal. Not even one newspaper in the United States saw fit to review a book that had the word *Freemasonry* on the front cover, not even in my hometown. The publisher was incredulous. "Even if a book is a tedious volume about how to prune Armenian begonias," he told me, "it gets a mention in the author's own local paper." But not in my case. The publisher sent a local book editor a press release, and then a copy of the book. He finally called the editor person-to-person, to be told, "I just don't think our readership would be interested in this subject."

Libraries disagreed. They apparently get a lot of calls for books about Masonry, and they became the first major purchasers. The book was reviewed in trade journals such as *Publishers Weekly* and *Kirkus Reviews*, and their positive reviews did result in a few bookstores stocking *Born in Blood*. As the publisher and I tried to comfort each other with that, neither of us could even fantasize that within two years over fifty thousand copies would be sold here and abroad.

It started with the idea of sending copies of the book to Masonic publications. One helpful soul tried to save us the expense, advising against the effort with the comment, "You'll have to learn that Masons don't read books." (What I learned is that some advice is best ignored.) I was gratified that many of the Grand Lodge publications recommended *Born in Blood* to their readers, but some took the opposite stand. I had not expected the book to arouse the controversy among Masons that it did in the beginning. Since respected Masonic scholars had stated in print that the true origins of Freemasonry were completely unknown, and that theories such as the birth of the Craft in medieval stonemasons' guilds were impossible to prove, I had thought that a new theory of Masonic origins would be welcome. Instead, I was attacked by many for "shallow research" and poor writing. ("It will put you to sleep," said one furious letter to a Masonic journal.)

One angry man went so far as to demand of his research lodge that *Born in Blood* be banned by the lodge and declared forbidden reading for Freemasons. I was gratified at what happened next, as the Master of the lodge refused to allow the motion, on the grounds that no Masonic body tells its members what they may or may not read.

Nor would any Masonic body participate in the suppression of any book. Now *that* was more in keeping with the opinion I had already formed about the Craft.

Then a letter came to my publisher from Richard Fletcher, executive secretary of the Masonic Service Association, who had been sent an advance copy. He graciously pointed out several factual errors (which were corrected in the second printing), such as President Reagan's membership being only honorary, and the settlement in 1984 of differences between the Grand Lodge of Utah and the Mormon Church. He made it clear that he did not agree with every point of my hypothesis, but he did say one thing that warmed my heart: "Mr. Robinson shows an understanding of us that we find rare indeed." That was a comforting thought while being tossed on the sea of controversy through which I found myself moving.

I shall never forget the first favorable Masonic review, which appeared in *The Philalethes* magazine under the byline of Allen Roberts. I had already come to identify Mr. Roberts as the most prolific Masonic author, perhaps in all of Masonic history, and his magazine commentaries gave substantial evidence that he was a man who would express his opinion, whether or not it was popular. I was greatly relieved to read his appraisal of *Born in Blood*, and could not resist calling him that same evening to express my thanks. What I thought would be a short call led to a half-hour conversation that sparked a friendship that is still very important to me. Allen Roberts gave a great boost to my prior conclusion that Freemasons would be fair-minded.

How far they would go to be fair was driven home to me by two events that still linger warmly in the forefront of my mind.

One day I received a phone call from a man who introduced himself as the managing editor of the *Scottish Rite Journal*, the official publication of the Southern Jurisdiction. His name was Dr. John Boettjer. He said that he was faced with a problem for which he had a solution, but he felt that the solution should have my approval. That alone surprised me, but he went on to explain that the magazine's book reviewer had submitted a negative review of *Born in Blood*. On the other hand, he had received letters praising the book from a number of Scottish Rite Masons. In fairness, he felt that he should run not one but two reviews, presenting both points of view. Dr. S. Brent Morris who had written the negative review had already wholeheartedly approved the idea of letting both sides have their say. What did I think of that plan?

What did I think? I thought that only a Masonic publication could come up with an approach so dedicated to fair-mindedness. All editors know that a movie or book review simply reflects the opinion of one person, but that doesn't bother them. Here was an editor who cared! I approved his plan, with gratitude.

The double review appeared in the *Scottish Rite Journal* under the heading "Thumbs Up—Thumbs Down," to my knowledge a journalistic first.

The other event involved the staff of the *Northern Light*, the monthly magazine of the Scottish Rite Northern Jurisdiction. The magazine's book reviewer had been harshly critical of *Born in Blood*, but by then I was learning to live with the fact that I can't please everyone. I only regretted that his opinion had gone out to almost half a million men.

Some months later, that book reviewer retired and was replaced by a younger man, Tom Jackson, who was also the Grand Secretary of Pennsylvania. The new reviewer approached the editor with the information that he regretted the original review, with which he disagreed. He wanted to write his own review of *Born in Blood*. It was an extraordinary suggestion, since it is rare that a publication would ever review the same book twice. Nevertheless, permission was granted and the new review appeared in *Northern Light*.

What was happening was that I was learning an important aspect of Freemasonry, the heart and soul of the fraternity that can't be found in bookish research in libraries, or recorded in dusty archives. I was meeting men to whom open-mindedness, fair-mindedness, and freedom of expression were a necessity of life. I was soon to learn much, much more from two avenues of education. One would give me the chance to talk with thousands of Freemasons; the other provided ample opportunity to discuss Masonry with the general public all across the country. I followed the two paths almost simultaneously, and sometimes they intertwined, but talking to Freemasons came first.

It started when I dropped by the Masonic Temple in Cincinnati to leave an autographed book, to express my gratitude to the man who had permitted me to use their extensive library for my research. As we renewed acquaintance, he introduced me to his boss, H. Ray Evans, the secretary of the Scottish Rite Valley of Cincinnati (and later Grand Master of the Masons of Ohio). The three of us had a great discussion for about half an hour, and then Mr. Evans asked me a question that was to launch me into a totally new experience: "Can you come here Thursday evening to talk to the Valley of Cincinnati?" I accepted readily, without telling him how flattered I was, nor how nervous I felt at the prospect.

That meeting set the stage for a format that has worked very well from the outset. I talked for just about twenty minutes, then invited comments, criticisms, and questions from the floor. That may be when my real Masonic education began. (I remembered an old piece of sound wisdom: "You never learn anything when your mouth is open.") And soon after becoming a first-time published author I found myself a first-time public speaker.

Alfred Rice, the Scottish Rite deputy for Ohio, was there at that first meeting, and at the end of the evening he invited me to speak at the Ohio Council of Deliberation, their state convention, a few weeks later at Youngstown. Men I met there invited me to come to Cleveland, Canton, and Steubenville.

How the word got around I don't know, but I found myself addressing Masonic bodies ranging from small lodges with seven or eight men present to Templar Commanderies, Scottish Rite Valleys, and Grand Lodges. The most memorable invitation came from the Grand Master of New Jersey. I met him at a reception, and at one point he asked me sternly: "What's the deal to get you to come to the Grand Lodge of New Jersey?" "Well, first, " I replied, "I never charge a fee. Second . . ." "That's enough!" the Grand Master interrupted. "You've already met all of our criteria." We both laughed, and another friendship was launched.

Another first for me was the invitation to participate in a church service. It was in Washington, D.C., during the Triennial Conclave of the Grand Encampment of Knights Templar. Then, a few weeks after returning to Washington to speak to the Grand Lodge of the District of

Columbia, I was overwhelmed by an invitation to act as the chairman of a workshop at the annual conference of Grand Masters. As though that wasn't honor enough, I was also asked to participate in the Scottish Rite, Southern Jurisdiction leadership conferences in Atlanta, Kansas City, and Denver.

Not all of the value to me lay in the question-and-comment sessions in the meetings. Every bit as enriching were the conversations with individuals and groups of Freemasons who gathered in the lobbies, restaurants, and lounges before and after those meetings. They shared their concerns and their ideas. They explained why they disagreed with points I had made and listened patiently while I explained how I had reached certain conclusions. We talked about problems of individual lodges, and I was surprised to learn that many men in leadership positions had not crossed the thresholds of their own neighborhood lodges for ten or fifteen years. They told me about their local charitable projects. I learned more than I had ever expected to know about Masonry. (I have also learned to carry less and less luggage down those long airport corridors.)

The experience of talking to the general public about Freemasonry came about through the medium of call-in radio and TV shows, and it started within my own family. My brother-in-law, knowing of my disappointment at being ignored by newspapers, took it upon himself to call a local radio station to suggest that I appear as a guest. The host of the show later told me that he had agreed because he had always been curious about Masonry because of the bad things he had been told about it as a youngster in a Catholic school. On the air, the calls poured in.

I had been assured by several Masons that the public had no interest in Freemasonry, and that there was no point in trying to spread the word because no one wanted to hear it. I don't know where that notion came from, but over the months ahead I would learn that the concept of public indifference to Masonry is totally, completely wrong. As the word spread, invitations to appear on radio and TV shows came in from all across the nation. People everywhere were curious about Freemasonry, and many were eager to call in to express their own opinions.

Non-Masons frequently have wrong impressions of Masonry, of course, but that is hardly surprising. The only voices many of them hear are those of anti-Masonic evangelical pundits pitching the sale of their books, pamphlets, audiotapes and even videotapes. Bigotry is big business for evangelists, although their usual source of income is limited to their own followers. Fortunately, the thinking public still outnumbers those who elect to have someone else do their thinking for them.

Sometimes the activities of speaking inside and outside the fraternity came together. On a trip to speak to the Grand Lodge of Florida, the committee arranged for me to appear on both a radio and TV station in the Tampa market. I went to Denver a full day before the opening of the Scottish Rite leadership conference at which I was to speak in order to be on a one-hour morning call-in radio show, then went to Colorado Springs to appear on a TV news broadcast, then had a fifteen-minute interview on a business radio network show syndicated to eighty cities. At the end of the broadcast day, I was interviewed by the *Rocky Mountain News*. A busy day, but one full of opportunities to talk about the language-disorder clinics supported by Scottish Rite Masons, a wonderful children's program that had been born right there in Denver. I have no idea what the total nationwide audience was but I do know that I no longer listen to anyone who says that there is no point in trying to carry the Masonic story to the general public because they just don't care. The truth is that most people don't know enough to care one way or the other. But they are curious, and very willing to listen.

As to what they have to say, and the opinions that some have formed about the Craft, and what Freemasons themselves have to say—that's what the rest of this book is all about.

The first part of the book primarily discusses radio and television contact with the general public and with the anti-Mason evangelists who currently seek to destroy Freemasonry totally. The second part is the result of my contacts with Masons, mostly drawn from appearances before Masonic bodies that involved over seventy-five thousand miles of air travel in 1992 alone.

The final chapter sums up my findings and feelings after all of those years of investigation into Freemasonry in America.

Part One

2

What Is a Mason?

I T'S A VERY simple question, but one commonly asked on radio
call-in shows. The station carries advance announcements that
there will be a program "about the Masons." At the opening of
the show the host will announce, "Today, we're going to talk about the
Masons." Then when calls start coming in, almost always someone
will ask, "Just what *is* a Mason?"

And then questions will flow that indicate a high level of public
interest or curiosity, backed by pitifully meager information.

"What's the difference between the Masons and the Freemasons?"

"I usually hear someone referred to as a '32nd degree Mason,'
but are there other kinds?"

"Is there any truth to what I've heard—that the Shriners are
somehow tied in with the Masons?"

"I think my grandfather was a Mason. I know that he had a
uniform with a sword and a big plume on his hat. What was he?"

"I've heard that they swear to kill any Mason who breaks his
oath. Isn't that against the law?"

"My pastor says that the Masons have their own religion. What
is it?"

"Why do Masons call their buildings 'Temples'?"

"The Masons have an orphanage here. Do they just take in the orphaned children of other Masons?"

"Why do the Masons have secret meetings? Are they afraid people will find out what they're really doing?"

"What is a Prince Hall Mason?"

"If I wanted to become a Mason, how would I go about it? How much does it cost?"

"Someone at work told me that the Masons worship Satan. Is that true?"

And the questions could go on page after page. Most people lack even rudimentary knowledge of the Masonic fraternity, which makes them prime targets for those eager to hand out misinformation. Most organizations feel the need for public information offices – as do even religions and governments – but Freemasonry has traditionally regarded itself as a private fraternity that does not need or desire to disseminate information or increase public awareness.

That situation appears to be changing, but a centralized information service will be difficult to implement, since there is no national governing body. To understand why, since not every reader of this book can be expected to be a Mason, it may be helpful to look at the structure of Freemasonry in the United States.

No matter where a man fits in the complex system of Freemasonry, he can only have entered Masonry in the basic local Masonic lodge, of which there are over thirteen thousand in the United States. The local lodge is sometimes called a "blue lodge," for reasons long lost, while others refer to it as a "symbolic lodge" (the term I will use in this book). The symbolic lodge confers just three degrees: the entrant, or Entered Apprentice, the Fellow Craft, and the Master Mason. Not until he is a Master Mason can a member join any of the other aspects of the fraternity. There are about five million Master Masons throughout the world, of whom about half are in this country.

In the rest of the world the Masonic fraternity is often governed by a single Grand Lodge for the whole country, such as the United Grand Lodge of England. American Masonry grew during the American Revolution, which was fought collectively by thirteen colonies, each of which thought of itself not as a province, but as a separate country, a sovereign *state*. When the colonies put together a common meeting ground for what would be called the United States of America, most of them used the term "state" in that sense of a sovereign power. Strictly speaking, they didn't have a *union*, but rather a cooperative agreement to deal with matters of common interest. That agreement was called the Articles of Confederation, which bestowed little authority on the central body. The Freemasons in each of the states felt similarly inclined to govern themselves.

As the weaknesses of the confederation manifested themselves, a growing party opted for stronger central control. The final result of their efforts, years later, was the Constitution of the United States, ratified only after months of angry debate and compromise, most of which stemmed from the problem of giving up authority to a central control.

The Freemasons did not make that change in their own administration, choosing rather to have a Grand Lodge for each state, with no central governing body. In the Masonic tradition the Grand Lodge is supreme. There is no control above it, and no Grand Lodge can tell any other Grand Lodge what to do.

There was just one time when the United States came close to having a central Grand Lodge. Back in 1779, while his army was in winter quarters, Freemason George Washington was approached by the American Union (Military) Lodge, saying that they wanted to propose him as the General Grand Master of Masons for the whole country. The nearby Grand Lodge of Pennsylvania agreed. Had Washington expressed any enthusiasm for the position, it would undoubtedly have been his, and today there would be a Grand Lodge of the United States. As it is now, it is highly unlikely that this country will ever have a Master Grand Lodge, especially since several Grand Lodges are now in serious disagreement about the wisdom of changing any aspect of ancient ceremonies.

By no means are all the Grand Lodges in the rest of the world free of material disagreements with each other. In most cases, the Grand Lodges may "agree to disagree," as on a point of ceremony or on meeting rules. The only disciplinary action available in the event of a serious dispute is for one Grand Lodge to simply decline to "recognize" the other. This usually means cutting off visitation rights (the right of a Mason to attend a meeting of a lodge other than his own), between the lodges involved and rejecting any common effort of any kind.

In the case of the Grand Orient (Grand Lodge) of France in the late nineteenth century, a dispute arose when the Grand Orient declared that it would accept atheists as members, in direct violation of what is probably the most fundamental membership requirement: a professed belief in God. In response, the Grand Orient was disavowed and declared clandestine by all the Grand Lodges of Great Britain, Canada, and the United States. So was the Prussian Grand Lodge rejected when it decided to stop admitting Jews. That decision against Jewish membership was quickly withdrawn by the Berliners, who preferred to abandon their prejudices in favor of re-establishing their worldwide fraternal recognition.

That recognition is exactly what is being sought by separate Masonic lodges maintained by about a quarter of a million black Americans. The organization is called Prince Hall Masonry, after its founder.

Prince Hall was a free black living in Boston, where he and fourteen of his black friends were made Freemasons in 1775 by a traveling military lodge, No. 441, of the British 38th Regiment of Foot. The Revolutionary War broke out soon after their initiation, and Prince Hall is said to have fought with the army of the rebelling colonists. The war pulled the British regiment out of the Boston area, leaving its black brothers behind.

The regiment and its Masonic lodge never did come back to Boston, and the local American Masonic lodges showed no desire to take in the black Masons, so Prince Hall finally made application to the Grand Lodge in England for a charter to a new lodge. After much delay, it was issued on September 29, 1784, authorizing the formation of African Lodge No. 459.

African Lodge was not welcomed by the other American lodges, and its efforts to stay in communication with the English Grand Lodge were unavailing. Ultimately, it declared itself an independent Grand Lodge (much as the American lodges had done during the Revolutionary War) and began warranting other lodges for African-Americans. It even warranted military lodges, which existed within black military units in the Civil War (although they are never even mentioned in the much-acclaimed movie and television shows about those units). It even expanded into appendant degrees, in much the same manner as white Masonry, which had condemned the black Prince Hall Masonic system as "clandestine," or unauthorized.

When I began looking into Masonry, not one single Grand Lodge had given its recognition to the Prince Hall Masons, a status which would grant visitation rights and permit both systems to clasp hands in brotherhood. That's what the Prince Hall Masons want—not a merger, which they do not favor, but the recognition that removes that denigrating "clandestine" status.

Times are changing, and as I write this, eight state Grand Lodges in the United States have extended that recognition to Prince Hall, as have two Grand Lodges in Canada. The subject is still controversial, but everyone, including the Masons, is learning to live with change. And "universal brotherhood" is a strong teaching of the Master Mason's initiation lectures.

In Masonic tradition, a man can get no "higher" than his status as a Master Mason. Therefore, the other Masonic systems are never called "higher" orders, but are designated "appendant." All of these appendant orders were created after Freemasonry revealed itself in London in 1717, and many of them function in just one country. Although there are numerous orders, the two best known which are open to a Master Mason in America are the York Rite and the Scottish Rite.

The York Rite order has a system of advancement that culminates in the York Rite Mason being made a Knight Templar. There are about two hundred and fifty thousand York Rite Templars in the United States. Even more popular is the system known as Scottish Rite, which has two separate sovereign territories. The Northern Jurisdiction covers fifteen states in the northeastern United States. The Southern Jurisdiction covers the other thirty-five states.

These Masonic bodies are totally separate, and neither the Northern nor the Southern Jurisdiction has any authority or control over the other. Each Jurisdiction determines independently the ritual dramas it performs in connection with each degree awarded, although both award degrees from the 4th through the 32nd—the latter being the degree most familiar to non-Masons. Both Jurisdictions award a 33rd degree, which is not earned for having completed a given body of work and learning but is bestowed for meritorious service. There are approximately one million Scottish Rite Masons in North America.

Once a man has achieved the status of York Rite Knight Templar, or Scottish Rite 32nd degree Mason, he may apply for membership in the Ancient Arabic Order of the Nobles of the Mystic Shrine and become a Shriner. The Shrine, which numbers about three quarters of a million members, also accepts eligible Masons in Canada and Mexico. (If we rearrange the initials A. A. O. N. M. S., they turn into "A Mason.")

The Shrine was founded as an organization dedicated to having fun, which led to local Shrine groups forming brass bands, oriental bands, bagpipe bands, motor patrols, motorcycle patrols, horse patrols, and the famous Shrine clown units—and that list doesn't cover them all. Over time, the dedication to personal enjoyment took a more serious turn, and the outcome was the twenty-two free Shrine hospitals for burned and crippled children, a great charity that earns praise everywhere. These unique medical centers, combined with Shrine parades and circuses, and Shriners wearing their red fezzes in public, have made the Shrine far and away the most visible aspect of American Masonry. Not so visible is the Shrine's Masonic roots. In talking to non-Masons across the country, I have rarely come across one who knows that every Shriner is also a Master Mason.

Another aspect of Freemasonry that is frequently misunderstood is the popular Order of the Eastern Star. This is not a "Masonic" order in the sense that it is part of Freemasonry, but it is made up of men and women with a Masonic connection. Men who join must be Master Masons. A woman who joins must be the wife, mother, sister, daughter, or granddaughter of a Master Mason. About eight hundred thousand men belong, and well over a million women. With that total membership of over two million, Eastern Star is easily the largest "coed" fraternal society in the world. To the best of my knowledge, Eastern Star has the approval of every Grand Lodge in the United States both for its aims and its charitable activities.

There are other related bodies, and among them are the Order of Demolay, for young men ages thirteen to twenty-one, Job's Daughters, and Rainbow for Girls. Members of those groups do not have to have a family connection to Freemasonry, but they do enjoy Masonic sponsorship and assistance.

Most important of all to an understanding of Freemasonry, perhaps, is an understanding of what its members believe and of their avowed purposes. It is, apparently, very confusing for non-Masons to learn that Freemasonry doesn't tell men what they are supposed to believe. Rather, the fraternity attracts men who already adhere to a set of beliefs about the nature of God, their relationship with Him, and the moral conduct their God requires.

The most important common ground of Freemasons is asserted before they ever become members of the fraternity, before they take part in any ceremony, before they take any oath. That common ground is established when a man applies for membership. The application, or "petition," signed by the candidate affirms that he believes in God and in the immortality of the soul.So when anyone meets a Mason, he can be certain that he is talking to a God-fearing man. Among the first words a new Freemason hears are that how he worships God is his own business, that how his Masonic brothers choose to worship God is *their* business, and that there will be no discussion of religion in his Masonic lodge. No Mason is to criticize any brother's religious convictions or try to persuade him to change them. Clearly then, every Freemason believes in freedom of religion.

That belief has allowed Freemasonry to become a system that permits men of all religious faiths to come together, to meet, to mix, to work together on projects that will benefit the whole community. Each Mason shares the belief that charity and love are in keeping with the wishes of his God, whether he calls his God Jehovah, Yahweh, or Allah.

It is important to Freemasons that the great coming together of men of all creeds must take place in an atmosphere of dedication to common standards of moral behavior. Each applicant is investigated by a lodge committee before the first degree is granted. How does this man treat his family? What is his pattern of behavior in his neighborhood and workplace? Has he ever had problems with the law? Will he fit into a fraternal society based on a strong sense of right and wrong? Once a man is inside the lodge as a Freemason, the importance of moral conduct as a condition of ongoing membership is repeatedly emphasized.

The fundamental ritual of Masonry centers on the building of the Temple of Solomon and on the fate of its master builder, so the lodge has become infused with the tools and symbols of the medieval stonemason. The traditional masons' tools—the square, compasses, setting maul, plumb line, and so on—are used to illustrate points of moral behavior. Some of those lessons have entered the language with such Masonic terminology as "on the level" and "on the square."

With over five million members, unsuitable men undoubtedly slip through the screening process. Some members will fail to live up to the standards they followed at the time they joined the fraternity and become guilty of conduct that would have barred them from membership in the first place. Masonic teaching advises that a man who seems to be straying from decent behavior be approached privately, to be questioned or admonished.

For those who stray too far there is provision for indictment, investigation, and a hearing. Minor offenders may be suspended for periods of time based on the gravity of the offense. Serious offenders may be ejected from Freemasonry. Some men meet that fate and become embittered. Masons know that such a man may become an aggressively vocal anti-Mason, sometimes willing to help other anti-Masons by twisting the truth of his won Masonic experience, or engaging in outright lies to "get even" with the brotherhood that would not tolerate his behavior. Others who follow that path were not ejected but resigned in anger because they had not prevailed in some issue, or were not elected by their brothers to a coveted post. Their numbers are very few, but their voices can be very loud.

It is important to understand that Freemasonry does not *teach* a man to believe in God, or in religious freedom, or in moral conduct, or in acts of charity. He must bring those beliefs with him into the brotherhood, where he will find them encouraged and reinforced. George Washington, Benjamin Franklin, and Paul Revere were not taught to love liberty in their Masonic lodges. They joined because the beliefs they already cherished were shared by other Masons and encouraged by the brotherhood. They became Masons in order to be with like-minded men.

Any man who joins a Masonic lodge expecting to learn the true pathway to God will be disappointed. He will hear no description of heaven, no description of hell, nor will he be handed a prescription for salvation. He must learn about such things from his minister, priest, or rabbi: They are not taught in the lodge.

The reason is simple: Religious differences drive men apart. They always have and always will, and so they work against the concept of a fraternity where men of common moral convictions, but disparate religious convictions, can meet to live and work together for the good of all.

Some will say, "If that's all they are doing, why do they have to do it in secret meetings? That makes me suspicious."

The difference between secrecy and privacy is in the eyes of the third party. Rumors came from a church in our city about the conflict between a minister and his congregation. There was obviously excitement in the air, but the general public didn't know why. Finally, an announcement was issued, saying that the minister had been asked to resign. A few weeks later, at a table with a local minister from a different church of that same denomination, curiosity made me ask just what the problem was that got the other minister fired. The answer came after a momentary pause, in the form of a question. "Are you a contributing member of our church?" When I answered that I was not, the minister replied, "Then you have no right to know. It is a private matter."

He was right, of course, and I changed the subject, but there are countless people who respect no privacy but their own. When they learn that something which has piqued their interest is none of their business, it only serves to intensify their curiosity and frequently arouses their suspicions as well.

Yes, the Freemasons do hold private meetings to conduct their own lodge business, but so do churches, government agencies, boards of education, and individual families. Privacy is a basic right in a free society (although we must admit that it is constantly being chipped away).

One might look at all this and say, "What's so unique about Freemasonry? Everyone believes in those things, don't they?" Does everyone believe in freedom of religion? No. In religious and ethnic tolerance? No. In every man's right to privacy? No. Individual freedom is a recent condition in human history and by no means universal, not even within the borders of our own country, where the greatest thrust to establish personal freedom in all of history was achieved.

So what does that have to do with Masonry? It takes a little knowledge of American history, and of the role of Freemasons in that history, to find the complete answer to that question. Without the answer, one cannot grasp the full importance, purpose, and contributions of Freemasonry in America.

It took me a while to see it, because originally I didn't know anything about Masons in American history. My motivation came from questions put to me that I felt I couldn't fully answer, and from debates with anti-Masonic evangelists that taught me that I should dig a bit deeper and think a little harder.

What I found was exciting. It enhanced my feelings about the fraternity and its value to society. Most Masons already know what I had "discovered," but for those who do not I'd like to pass on what I learned, an important step to understanding just what Masons are and what they believe.

3

The Fountainhead of Freedom

WHEN I FIRST began to take questions from the public about Freemasonry, I usually gave quick and superficial answers to the questions, "What is Masonry all about?" and "What do Masons stand for?" I would simply repeat what I had frequently been told: "It's a fraternal society dedicated to self-improvement and charitable works."

With more research and a little reasoning, I realized that I had been giving a totally inadequate definition. Freemasonry is much more than self-improvement and charitable acts. It has made a great impact on all our lives, and upon the world, by drawing upon a statement of purpose that I had previously not fully comprehended, because I had not clearly seen the Masonic impact on the formation of this country.

That purpose rests in the admonitions given to the new Entered Apprentice. He has fulfilled the major Masonic requirement of attesting to his belief in God and immortality, and now he is told that no Mason is permitted to violate any brother's right to total religious privacy. Within the lodge, he is not to criticize, proselytize, or mock the faith of any other person.

That seems straightforward enough: Freemasons believe in freedom of religion. The unusual aspect is that Freemasonry had practiced that principle long before there was a United States of America, or a Bill of Rights. The events that unfolded to make the thirteen British colonies a separate nation, and the men who led those events, point to a very strong contribution by Freemasons, an historic fact that is not even whispered to students of American history.

As children, we were taught that many beleaguered religious groups came to the colonies in search of freedom of worship. What we were *not* taught was that those groups usually came here in search of religious freedom for themselves alone, but not for anyone else. There was little freedom of religion across the thirteen colonies. When Roger Williams fled religious persecution to found the colony of Rhode Island, he was not fleeing persecution in Europe, but in Massachusetts. He built a Baptist church there that functioned in an atmosphere of religious tolerance. Rhode Island, and perhaps Quaker-dominated Pennsylvania, were to be the only colonies to come even close to our twentieth-century concept of religious freedom.

Each other colony had its own state religion, with the right to tax its citizens for the support of that denomination. Connecticut, for example, was Congregationalist, while the colony of Virginia, mother of presidents and a birthplace of freedom, was militantly Church of England. Laws on the books of Virginia called for the public flogging of ministers of other denominations who dared to preach "nonconformist" sermons to their congregations. Those persecutions drove many Baptist and Methodist congregations to pack their wagons and leave Virginia for the wilderness of the Southeast.

In such an atmosphere, how did the Founding Fathers come up with the idea of a new country that would have no state religion, leaving all men to worship God as they saw fit? There was no role model in any nation on the face of the earth. Rulers were convinced that a state religion was absolutely necessary for the orderly administration of the people. Did the champions of the Bill of Rights create their ideas out of thin air, with no source of inspiration? Not likely.

Actually, there *was* one source, a source well known to influential men in all thirteen colonies, a teaching that crossed all boundaries. That lesson was taught in all their Masonic lodges, an organization that alone had pioneered a way for all God-fearing men to meet in brotherhood. Can that source of this nation's religious freedom be conclusively proven? Of course not, but it gains strength from the fact that there is no alternate source available. In all the world, only Freemasons espoused that doctrine.

Consider the diverse nature of the men who had embraced the Masonic philosophy. Today, we lump them together as "patriots," but they differed in their education, occupation, and social background. Paul Revere was a silver craftsman. John Hancock was a merchant. George Washington was a wealthy planter. John Warren, who died leading his men at Bunker Hill, was a medical doctor. John Paul Jones was a Scottish seaman. Benjamin Franklin was a printer, the Marquis de Lafayette a French nobleman. What did these, and hundreds of other patriots, have in common? Nothing, except that they were all Freemasons. They were attracted to Freemasonry because its philosophy of individual freedom matched their own convictions. It gave them a common bond and a gathering place for the meeting of minds that they otherwise would not have. Perhaps it was no coincidence that in Philadelphia in 1775, while the local Masonic lodge conducted its business on the upper floor of Tun Tavern, their Masonic brother Samuel Nicholas was seated at a table on the ground floor, encouraging men to sign up for a totally new colonial military force, to be called the Corps of Marines. Appointed to the rank of captain, Brother Nicholas became the first commandant of the Marine Corps.

No one should be surprised that the Freemasons feel a special involvement with the American Revolution. On the military side Freemasons Washington, Jones, and Nicholas commanded the army, navy, and marines. Off at the distant frontier, their Masonic brother George Rogers Clark led a force of Kentucky pioneers and woodsmen hundreds of miles across rivers, through deep woods, and across a treacherous swamp to take the British forts of Kaskaskia, Cahokia, and Vincennes.

The senior statesman of the Revolution, Benjamin Franklin, drew on the help of his Masonic brothers in France to gain audiences at the French court to seek assistance against a common enemy. The legend persists that a meeting of St. Andrew's Lodge in Boston was cut short to give the members ample time to join the Boston Tea Party; disguised as Indians, they hurried to the harbor to throw the tea overboard. Some say it is more than mere legend: The original minutes of that evening's business indicate a very short meeting. Masons like to remember the Junior Deacon of that lodge, Paul Revere, waiting in the darkness beside his horse. He was watching anxiously for one of his Masonic brothers to hang one lantern or two in the tower of the Old North Church, so that he could ride off to warn the neighboring rebels of the approach route of the British troops.

As exhilarating as the military achievements may have been, they were events of the moment. The true value of victory in war can only be measured by how it is used. Rebellion was not new to the world, but its usual purpose was to replace one ruler with another. This was the first major attempt to wrest control from one ruler and place it in the hands of the people.

The Bill of Rights amendment saying that the national government would not embrace a state religion had a double purpose. One was to make certain that democratic government by the people could not be stripped away by any autocratic religious hierarchy, as had happened so often around the world. The other was to provide the greatest latitude for the worship of God. There can be no true democracy without freedom of religion.

There is no way to estimate precisely the influence of Freemasonry on this entire process, but it would be foolish not to acknowledge that it was significant. Throughout the Western world, revolutionary leaders who determined to throw off the oppressive control of church and state turned to Freemasonry as a way to join with others who shared their beliefs. Benito Juárez, the full-blooded Oaxaca Indian who had determined to throw off the yoke that enslaved the people of Mexico, became a Freemason.

Simon Bolívar became a Mason in London, where he appealed for help from his new Masonic brothers for his revolution in South America. The Knights Templar of England, a Masonic body commanded by the duke of Sussex—who was also Grand Master of the newly-formed United Grand Lodge of England—arranged to send training officers and supplies. Colonel Beresford, a Freemason sent to serve as Bolívar's chief training officer, later became a general and second-in-command to another Freemason, the duke of Wellington, in the Peninsular Campaign against the forces of the dictator

Napoleon Bonaparte. The other great South American revolutionary, General José de San Martín, also joined the Masonic fraternity. All the Hispanic revolutionary leaders earned the enmity of the Vatican for stripping the Roman Church of lands and political power, and especially for drying up the steady stream of income that had previously flowed into the Vatican treasury.

The revolutionary leader who angered the Church leaders most of all was the Sicilian Giuseppe Garibaldi. While living in the self-imposed exile necessary for his personal safety, Garibaldi became a Freemason at a lodge in Staten Island, New York. He returned to his homeland, and this time led a successful campaign to unify Italy under King Victor Emmanuel II.

Now the church had lost not only property and income, but also the pope's status as a secular ruler, complete with tax gatherers, courts, prisons, and a standing army. Clearly, it was this crushing blow that compelled Pope Leo XIII to issue the most scathing condemnation ever of Freemasonry, the 1884 encyclical entitled *Humanum Genus*. Taking the stand that has become the party line of Christian fundamentalists everywhere, Leo declared that the followers of the One True Religion made up the Kingdom of God, while all non-Catholics belonged to the Kingdom of Satan. The Freemasons were condemned as leaders of these non-Catholic Satanists, not on theological grounds, but for their support of the basic tenets of democracy. The tenet Leo hated most was that of the separation of church and state:

> They [the Masons] work, indeed obstinately, to the end that neither the teaching nor the authority of the Church may have any influence; and therefore they preach and maintain the full separation of the Church from the State. So law and government are wrested from the divine virtue of the Catholic Church, and they want, therefore, by all means to rule States independent of the institutions and doctrines of the Church.

Freedom of speech is not overlooked for condemnation, because it permits people to criticize the Church without punishment:

> Full license is given to attack with impunity, both by
> words and print and teaching, the very foundations of
> the Catholic religion; the rights of the Church are
> violated; her divine privileges are not respected.

Despite the pope's protest, the truth is that the Masons do not preach, teach, or insist on the doctrine that church and state should be separate, although it appears to follow logically from their teaching of the right to freedom of worship. It certainly seems to be necessary if government is truly intended to be in the hands of all the people.

Not even dictatorships have their won way when they recognize a state religion. In 1929, when Mussolini desperately wanted the support of the Catholic Church for his new regime, he negotiated the Lateran Treaty, familiarly know to Italians as the *Concordat*. In that treaty Mussolini agreed that Italy would have no laws that did not adhere to church teachings. He gave the Church veto power over much of the government, which agreed to forbid divorce. The Church also controlled the schools, the libraries, and the publishing business, and even had the authority to exercise control over which books, magazines, and newspapers could be imported into the country.

I had my first brush with that type of control when I discovered the writings of Tom Paine during World War II. I had known of his general influence on events leading to the American Revolution, but had never experienced for myself the clarity and fervor of his writing. Eager to discuss the work with someone else, I handed my paperback copy of *The Rights of Man* to a good friend. I asked that he read it so that we could talk about it. He handed the book back to me saying, "You know I'm a Catholic. We're not permitted to read anything written by Thomas Paine." Until that moment, I had not known that any organization tried to control what people read.

More recently, in 1992, a fundamentalist Protestant church a few miles from my home announced a public book-burning of printed material offensive to God. it was to be open to the public because the minister of the church said that God had specifically instructed him to burn the books in view of all, and to alert the local media. He was to burn material that taught moral lessons without Jesus (including such stories as "The Ant and the Grasshopper" and "The Tortoise and the Hare"), because such non-Christian moral teachings, usually identified as "secular humanism," are offensive to God. The fire received anything the church could find published by "condemned" groups, such as Christian Scientists, Mormons, Unitarians, and Seventh-day Adventists. (As I read the newspaper accounts, I could not resist asking myself, "Can *Kristallnacht* be far behind?")

We must understand that such stands by certain religious leaders—preposterous as they may appear—are often the result of a sincere desire to do God's will. If a man is totally convinced that his faith alone has been given the divine seal of approval, then he considers that it is his duty to reveal the truth of God's words according to his own faith and to point to the path of salvation that only he can make plain. And it is obvious to him that if his faith is the One True Religion, all other religious faiths must be false, and offensive to God. He not only preaches the moral standards of his faith to his own followers, but feels compelled to inform the county, state, and federal governments as to which laws are and are not in conformity with God's will, which books God want us to read, what music He approves, which movies should be produced.

I listened to this thesis one day and said to the evangelist espousing it, "Aren't you really saying that you do not believe in the separation of church and state, freedom of religion, and freedom of speech?" He replied that the separation of church and state was an abomination. God cannot be separated from control of any human endeavor, especially the making and enforcing of laws. As for those individual freedoms, his faith taught total freedom for all people to act and speak in accordance with God's will. To want to act or speak otherwise was not an appeal for freedom, but an appeal for satanic license to thwart and corrupt the word of God.

This is the position taken by fundamentalists worldwide, not just fundamentalist Protestants. There are fundamentalist Catholics, fundamentalist Jews, fundamentalist Muslims. When operating in frustration as a minority, they labor incessantly to gain control. When they do gain control, the results can be devastating. Look at the Shi'ite fundamentalists who took control of every aspect of Iranian life and government under their fanatical leader, the Ayatollah Khomeini.

Following the path of all such dogmatic fundamentalist leaders, Khomeini promptly declared that his enemies (the people of the United States) worship Satan. Then he outlawed Freemasonry.

It was fundamentalist control of the Catholic Church that gave birth to the Inquisition, created to "purify" the One True Religion. In that period the Catholic leaders felt so confident that one pontiff could declare that, since every human being needed to be saved, then every human being on the face of the earth must be subject to the pope, who controlled the only pathway to salvation. It is the fundamentalists in the Middle East who gave birth to the terroristic brotherhoods and suicide squads. Historically, more blood has been spilled in the world for this narrow-visioned love of God than for the love of war.

Some political theorists of the past century decided that since control by men of God was so often tyrannical, the key to happiness must be the absence of God and religion from the community. The result was militant communism, which encouraged atheism, teaching it in the schools and requiring it of every party member. (Freemasons obviously do not agree, since no atheist can become a Mason.)

In spite of the brutal enforcement of an atheistic society, it just didn't work. Despite tight control over education, the press, and the legislature, millions of people would not abandon their love of God and their need for a spiritual faith. Children were taught in secret and the elderly were permitted to continue their religious observances on a limited basis, probably on the theory that they would soon die off. At a Muslim shrine in Central Asia, I saw a sign posted inside the shrine by the communist government that told the worshipers, "Praying to God is like asking that two plus two please not equal four." On a nearby school building another poster proclaimed, "Science is light, religion is darkness." Both were quotations from Lenin.

I prefer the democratic method of permitting all people to worship God as they see fit, so that all people can live together in freedom, including freedom from fear. That is one reason I have come to admire the principles of Freemasonry. It is trying hard to provide a way for all men to come together, limited only by the prohibition against atheists and the insistence on moral conduct.

Most of us grew up believing that religious tolerance is a good thing, but a recent book by a Southern Baptist zealot used the

Masons' attitude toward tolerance as a reason to condemn them as anti-Christian. God, according to the author, insists upon *intolerance*, so that any man or group of men "tolerating" men of diverse religions is the Antichrist.

A strange aspect of all this is that the histories of their own faiths, often written by fundamentalists, love to dwell on the abominable persecutions of their early predecessors, inflicted by the established universal church of the day. They don't see themselves as fighting hard to get into that same position, not to avoid persecution, but have the power to inflict it on anyone who refuses to toe the line they lay down.

The infamous Inquisition finds its way into so much religious history that some mention should be made of the changes that have taken place since then. The Catholic Church no longer brands every non-Catholic a follower of Satan, as Pope Leo XIII did in *Humanum Genus* a century ago. Nor does it still concur with that pontiff's condemnation of democracy. Great changes have taken place in attitudes, if not in specific teaching, under the influence of leaders such as Pope John XXIII. American Catholics, too, have exerted a great influence on church thinking, having lived for generations in a system that espouses individual rights and freedoms.

It would be foolish to say that America is now a land totally free of prejudices. The system tries to move people in that direction, but unfortunately a stream of leaders have found a path to wealth and power by fanning the flames of those prejudices. They miss no opportunity to pounce upon any item they can use to convince their followers to fear, to hate, and to fight. They are making certain that the conflicts will stay with us for a long time.

That's why it's easy to see Freemasonry as a haven of sanity and brotherhood. But that in turn makes it a frequent target of those leaders who wish to drive men apart, the better to control them and amass great wealth, not caring that they themselves are major deterrents to any hope of achieving universal brotherhood.

Sometimes trying to track the gains and losses of the battle for brotherhood is difficult. I sat in a meeting of the Grand Lodge of Vermont as a visiting officer of the Catholic Knights of Columbus expressed a desire to enhance the brotherhood of the two fraternities.

It was good to hear. But after the meeting one of the Vermont Masons told me that he had received a letter from his K.C. council telling him that he must resign from Masonry or he would be expelled from the Knights of Columbus. Still, I believe that there has been substantial progress. I frequently read of charitable projects sponsored jointly by Masons and K.C. members and, in one instance, of their pooling resources to build a common center for meetings of both orders.

This information, of course, will make some Protestant fundamentalists angrier than ever with Freemasonry, convinced as they are that Catholicism is also guilty of perverting God's truth.

One thing is very clear in all this. The fundamentalist leaders, who are so fond of reciting earlier persecutions of their church, absolutely refuse to acknowledge that Freemasonry had a major role in ending that persecution and in shaping a system of government that gives them complete freedom of expression. Rather than being grateful, they want Masonry destroyed. The tolerance that they so desperately needed to survive and to grow is now condemned as countering the will of God. Having been rescued and protected by others, they now feel strong enough to attack those who were their best friends at a time when they needed friends.

The anti-Masonic efforts have become such a threat that it will behoove every Mason to become familiar with their accusations, and to be prepared to respond. The allegations will get more complex, and specific, as they unfold. Many of them relate to one ancient and pervading charge, that Freemasonry is a separate religion. This charge has been answered a hundred times and more, but will not go away, as anti-Masons borrow twisted information from each other. It is that criticism of Masonry that should be addressed first.

4

Is Freemasonry a Religion?

’ve lost count of how many times I have been asked, “Isn’t
Freemasonry a separate religion?” It’s a question that creates a
question: “How in the world did anyone come to believe that
Masonry is a religion?” When I ask that, I am usually told by the
callers that they heard the charge on an evangelist’s broadcast, or
read it in an anti-Masonic tract or book. No one who has asked me the
question has claimed to have come up with the notion from personal
knowledge or experience.

The basic question has been addressed over and over again:
“No, Masonry is not a religion. It has no intention of being a religion.
It doesn’t *want* to be a religion.” But those replies rarely have any
impact on non-Masons for the simple reason that the defense of
Masonry is usually directed at other Masons, not at the masses who
are the targets of the anti-Masonic evangelists. What is obviously
needed is a broader audience for the defense.

One point that is confusing to many is the frequent statement by
Masonic writers that Freemasons are “religious.” They are, but being
religious in no way carries with it the concept of being part of a
separate religion. My own parents were very religious, but I really
don’t believe that they were a separate religion. Any minister of the

gospel will agree that he is religious, but every one will deny that he considers his teachings to be those of a separate religion.

Usually, the allegation that Masonry is a separate religion is helped along by one or more blatant falsehoods—for example, the charge that Masonry has its own path to salvation, through the performance of good works. I never met a Mason who believed that, or who would be able to understand how anyone could ever draw such a conclusion. In practice, it is a handy point for anti-Masons, who are frequently confronted with, "But if the Masons are such evil people, how do you explain their free hospitals, their language-disorder clinics for children, their eye-care program, their homes for the elderly, and all those other Masonic charities?"

The anti-Masonic answer comes back as, "The Masonic charities are not beloved of God because the Masons teach that good works are the way to salvation. That makes those charities against the will of God." That's sick, but it's what some of them say.

Masonry leaves it up to the individual Mason to choose his pathway to God, and that policy naturally includes no rules, advice, or admonitions as to the means of salvation. The Mason is expected, quite properly, to get that spiritual guidance from his own denomination, which he is encouraged to support with both his energy and his personal finances.

Time after time in various lectures, the Freemason is told *never* to put his duties and responsibilities to the Masonic fraternity ahead of his duties and responsibilities to his church, to his country, and to his family. As for Masonic charities, whether they are organized major efforts or individual acts of kindness (such as aid to a destitute brother, or to his widow and their children), the Mason is told to make no gift that will affect his duty to care for his own family.

In the ceremonies and lectures that lead to a man being raised to the status of Master Mason, he hears no description of heaven or hell. He hears no religious dogma. He hears no mention of Satan. He is told of no Masonic pathway to salvation for the simple reason that there is none.

The only religious item in the Masonic lodge is the holy book of the initiate's own faith. Since most Masons are Protestant Christians, that book is usually the King James version of the Bible. The initiate may be given a Masonic Bible by his lodge, his friends, or his family, but it varies from other editions of actual Scripture by not one single word. It is only a "Masonic" Bible because it also contains a brief history of Masonry, or a concordance to relate certain Masonic ritual to scriptural passages. Masons who are not Protestants bring their own holy books for their initiations.

Let's start at the beginning: When a man decides to become a Mason, based on what he has seen, heard, or experienced, he files an application, or "petition," with a local Masonic lodge. In signing that petition he asserts that he believes in God, the Supreme Being, and in the immortality of the soul. In the lecture accompanying the initiation rites of the first degree, called Entered Apprentice, he is told that how he chooses to worship God is up to his own conscience.

The religious experience in the lodge is prayer. Every meeting of Masons opens and closes with prayer. Every meal begins with prayer. As is done so often by the federal government (as, for example, with "In God we trust"), all prayer is addressed (or should be) to God the Father, so that a mixed audience of Christians, Jews, Muslims, and Buddhists, for instance, can relate that prayer to their own worship. Masons also offer prayers for charitable endeavors, for bereaved Masons and their families, or for a departed brother.

Clearly, one can easily assert that Freemasonry is not a separate religion. It promotes no heaven, no hell, and no means of salvation. There's no "witnessing" or arguing over religious beliefs in the lodge. There is no religious dogma. It *can't* be a religion.

Nevertheless, it is frequently charged that the Masonic lodge has its own God, whose name is "The Great Architect of the Universe." That Masonic term is not a name; it is a designation or reference, as are all terms beginning with the word "The": *The* Almighty, *The* Creator, *The* Most High. If it starts with "The," it is not a name. So why do the Masons use that designation?

Masonry, as its name implies, centers symbolically around the ancient builders of temples and cathedrals. It is natural for groups to fashion a designation for God that relates to their interests. In the military, I attended an outdoor church service conducted by a visiting chaplain, an ordained minister. He referred to God as "Our Supreme Commander-in-Chief in heaven." The Masons often do refer to God as

The Great Architect of the Universe, but what's wrong with that? The architect is one who plans and brings a structure into being. Historians refer to the Founding Fathers as the "architects of the Constitution." As a designation for God, The Great Architect of the Universe makes sense, and it means precisely the same thing as the universally popular "The Creator." The slight difference is that the Masonic designation implies that God created the world according to a plan, although there is no Masonic description of what that plan may be.

Then there is the charge that the third degree, that of Master Mason, teaches a Masonic resurrection. That is simply not true, and I have to believe that those who make that allegation are fully aware that it is not true. When, in debates, I have told people who trot out that charge that they are either ignorant of the truth, or deliberately lying, they tend to back off. They change the subject, rather than attempting to prove their point, which they know cannot be done. (Their own followers never demand that they prove anything.)

The act referred to in the allegation of resurrection is easily identified. In the initiation drama of the third degree, the master builder of Solomon's temple is murdered by three assassins, who hide the body in an obscure grave in the wilderness. By the time the grave is discovered, the body is decomposing. It is dug up and brought back to Jerusalem for a proper burial. Taking a body from one grave to put it in another is called "re-interment," or reburial. It meets no one's definition of *resurrection.*

A favorite charge is that Freemasonry *must* be a religion because it has a funeral service. The critics never mention that the Masonic service is *in addition* to the religious service, not in place of it. I have attended several Marine Corps funeral services that took place after the graveside religious service, and they offer a good comparison. The marines are usually in full dress uniform, and there is often a squad of men with rifles who fire a volley into the air above the open grave. The coffin is covered with an American flag. An officer or friend may deliver a prayer and eulogy for the deceased brother and commit his soul to a loving God. After the military tribute, the flag is removed from the coffin, folded in the traditional triangular shape, and formally presented to the nearest relative of the departed marine before the coffin is lowered and covered.

Does this mean that the Marine Corps is a separate religion? Of course not. It simply means that a departed brother is acknowledged and honored by a group of brothers-in-arms. Ask your local sheriff or policeman if he has ever attended a graveside service for a fallen law-enforcement officer. The police service is often conducted by a chaplain who may not be of the same faith as the deceased. Sometimes hundreds and even thousands of law-enforcement officers, who may never have met their fallen brother, will attend the ceremony, which is carried out *in addition* to the regular religious service. That is exactly the spirit of a Masonic funeral service, and I know from personal experience that wives, parents, and children appreciate the tribute paid to the loved one whom they mourn.

One anti-Masonic charge that really distorts the spirit of the fraternity arises from the fact that when a Mason takes the oath of loyalty to the Masonic brotherhood, the Masonic symbols of the square and compasses rest on top of the Holy Bible. To the Mason-hater, that clearly means that Freemasons put their order above God. If you go into a courtroom tomorrow and place your hand on top of the bible to take the oath to tell the truth, or to take an oath of office, does the higher position of your hand mean that you are putting yourself above God?

A reverse allegation is that the Masons *must* be the Antichrist because there are no symbols of Jesus in the lodge room. No, there are not. Nor are there symbols there of any other religion. They would not be appropriate to a fraternal society, especially one specifically espousing freedom of religion to the extent of admitting men of all faiths.

A more recent anti-Masonic allegation is based on the fact that the Masons teach lessons of morality which they illustrate with the tools of the medieval mason: for example, the square, the compasses, the setting maul, the level, and the plumb line. These lessons, relating to principles such as self-improvement, fair dealing, truthfulness, and charity, are objectionable to some religious leaders because morality is being taught without specific reference to Jesus. They call it "secular humanism." There is no way to answer that charge, because it is based on the concept that without Jesus there is no such thing as moral teaching. Since most of the world's population is not

Christian, we can only hope that position is wrong. All manner of secular societies encourage their members to live by moral codes, including the Campfire Girls, the Boy Scouts of America, 4-H clubs, the American Bar Association, and the American Medical Association (whose codes of ethics could easily be labeled "secular humanism"). As we look at the state of the society we live in today, it seems wise to endorse the teaching of moral behavior by any means whatsoever.

It may well be pointed out that I am not fully qualified to discuss this whole matter, since I am not a Freemason who has personally experienced Masonic ritual, nor am I a seminarian who has received specific training in Christian theology and bible studies. I could offer no rebuttal to such a charge. I can only suggest that we take a look at extracts from the written statements of several respected religious leaders who have had formal training in their subject. They are all Freemasons and have all passed through the three degrees of the symbolic lodge, and through the highest degrees of Scottish Rite. (All of these statements have appeared in the monthly journal of the Southern Jurisdiction of Scottish Rite):

> Freemasonry is not a religion, though in my experience, Masons have predominantly been religious men, and, for the most part, of the Christian faith.
>
> Freemasonry has no dogma or theology. It offers no sacraments. It teaches that it is important for every man to have a religion of his own choice and to be faithful to it in thought and action. As a result, men of different religions meet in fellowship and brotherhood under the fatherhood of God. I think that a good Mason is made even more faithful to the tenets of his faith by membership in the Lodge.
>
> REV. DR. NORMAN VINCENT PEALE, 33rd degree
> *1025 Fifth Avenue*
> *New York, New York*

> Let me quickly and emphatically say that Freemasonry is not and never has been a religion; however,

Freemasonry has always been a friend and ally of religion. In 50 years as a mason and as a minister, I have found no conflict between my Masonic beliefs and my Christian faith. I have not found and do not now find that Freemasonry is "incompatible with Christian faith and practice."

BISHOP CARL J. SANDERS, 33rd degree,
Grand Cross
United Methodist Church
Dothan, Alabama

Masonry is not a substitute for religion, nor is it a religion.

I am proud to be a Mason who believes in the freedom of mankind and the sanctity of human life.

I am proud to be a Mason who believes in the dignity of God's children and opposes hatred and bigotry, and stands for truth, justice, kindness, integrity and righteousness for all.

RABBI SEYMOUR ATLAS, 32nd degree
Beth Judah Synagogue
Wildwood, New Jersey

It is no secret that the Bible holds the central position as the great light of Masonry. It is no secret that Masons love and revere the Bible, nor is it a secret that Masonry helped to preserve it in the darkest age of the church when infidelity sought to destroy it.

It is no secret that high above Masonry's steeple is the ever-watchful and all-seeing eye of Almighty God.

Masonry respects every man's right to the religion of his choice and never claims or desires to be any man's religion nor a substitute for it.

DR. JAMES P. WESBERRY,
Exec. Director and Editor, SUNDAY
Georgia Baptist Center
Atlanta, Georgia

It should be understood that my discussion in this chapter has concerned itself with the basic three degrees of the local lodge: Entered Apprentice, Fellow Craft, and Master Mason. That is the experience shared by every Mason, so the references will be readily understood by all of them. In recent times, more scathing attacks have been launched against the appendant Masonic systems, such as York Rite and Scottish Rite, each of which is followed by a minority of Masons in this country. For that reason, it seems proper to address them separately, along with a look at some of the major anti-Masons of our own time — who usually quote the writings of Masons who have been dead for over a hundred years.

The long-dead Masonic writer who is most often cited is Albert Pike. Any attempt to understand the anti-Masonic movement currently being encouraged by fundamentalist evangelists requires a background knowledge of Pike and his work. He was an interesting man.

5

Albert Pike and the Morning Star

A LBERT PIKE (1809–91) was a lawyer, a poet, a prolific writer, a general in the army of the Confederate States of America, and a Freemason. He was a voracious reader, especially interested in the religions and philosophical systems of ancient cultures, which he saw as having shaped the thinking and codes of morality of people around the world. As a general, he commanded neither white nor black troops, but American Indians. He studied and respected their religious beliefs. But no matter how deeply he probed into other religions, nothing Pike learned ever shook his own faith as a devout Trinitarian Christian. Politically, he did not favor stronger central control, as is evidenced by his willingness to risk his life and fortune in a war that started not over the issue of slavery, but over the political concept of states' rights. In hindsight Pike may be judged to have been wrong politically, but at least he was willing to die for what he believed.

Fundamentalist anti-Masons love to condemn all Freemasonry based on the writings and philosophy of Albert Pike. They never say that Pike's works were written only for the Southern Jurisdiction of Scottish Rite Masonry, which was the limit of Pike's Masonic authority. He was the Sovereign Grand Commander of that Masonic body fro 1859 until his death in 1891.

The Southern Jurisdiction of Scottish Rite in America covers thirty-five southern and western states. It has about half a million members, or about 20 percent of the total Masonic membership in the United States. That means that about 80 percent of American Masons have little or no knowledge of the work of General Pike. I have found that most Masons have not even heard of him. These men are mystified by attacks on Masonry that cite Pike's writings, since they have no idea what the antagonist is talking about.

Pike's passion—perhaps obsession—was that all men should seek knowledge, or "light." From that light came information and understanding. Some fundamentalists, however, assert that all "light" comes from Jesus, and that any other source of light is anti-Christian, even though the rest of the world continues to use expressions like, "We've got to bring this to *light*," or, "Can anyone here shed some *light* on this matter?" That's what the Scripps-Howard newspaper chain had in mind when it adopted a lighthouse as its trademark, with the slogan, "Give the people light and they will find their way."

"Light," in the sense that is used by Pike, means education. Education is one of those things that most of us think is universally approved, but the anti-Masons take Masonry to task for such emphasis on it, taking the stand that too much secular education can be damaging to a good Christian. They often fall back on the belief of their predecessor fundamentalists of generations ago, who believed that education requires no written work other than Holy Scripture.

Yet that scripture itself admonishes Christians to seek knowledge, and totally supports the Masonic dedication to charity. Christian Masons can take comfort from the second epistle of Peter 1:5–7: "And beside this, giving all diligence, add to your faith virtue; and to virtue knowledge; And to knowledge temperance; and to temperance patience; and to patience godliness; And to godliness brotherly kindness; and to brotherly kindness charity." A good summary of Masonic belief.

Very few people are aware that in the lecture accompanying the second degree in the symbolic lodge all Masons are encouraged to continue their own education and to gain knowledge in the liberal arts, defined in the older context of that term as grammar, rhetoric, logic, arithmetic, music, astronomy, and geometry. The Masons emphasize the benefits of continuing education, even to the extent that many Masonic charities provide scholarships for deserving students on a nondenominational basis. Pike was in complete harmony with that approach, but he was somewhat different in that his own fascination was heavily weighted toward the history of religion, the subject of most of his writings.

Pike was convinced that he had benefited greatly from his lifelong studies of other religions and philosophies, because what he had learned gave him a broader understanding of all humankind. Many of the ancient religions he had studied were gone from the earth, but he was convinced that they had made contributions to later thought and moral systems. He had a good point: There are those who would deny that Muhammad learned anything from the Jews and Christians he met on his trading missions, or that Moses learned anything while growing up at the Egyptian court, but reason indicates the opposite.

Not everyone believes that familiarity with other religions and cultures is beneficial, however; exposure to alien ideas and customs may be thought to contaminate the student's religious and political beliefs. That's why the Catholic Church created the Index of books not to be read by Catholics, and why fundamentalists have sought the legal exclusion from classrooms and libraries of books that teach morality on a nonreligious basis, or even scientific knowledge that seems at odds with Scripture.

In his conviction that wisdom would be gained by learning what others believed, and why they behaved as they did, Albert Pike poured his prodigious knowledge into written works, so that he could share that information. Today, universities offer master's and doctoral degrees in the comparative study of world religions and in the history of religion. Pike would have approved. His plan was to educate all Scottish Rite Masons in his Southern Jurisdiction by imparting that comparative knowledge as an essential aspect of Scottish Rite training.

The course of education Pike laid out was in twenty-nine parts, to fit the Scottish Rite system of the 4th through the 32nd degrees.

Rather than being taught in pedantic lectures, the information is imparted primarily in ceremonial dramas, which are usually more effective in helping the student to retain what he has learned. The major difference between the Pike-inspired course of instruction and that employed in some theological seminaries is that Scottish Rite does not identify any religion as the One True Faith. It teaches to inform, not to prove the error of all faiths except that of the lecturer. Some of the work does arrive at conclusions, such as those condemning tyranny (from either a religious or secular source), and a charge to seek the light of knowledge, rather than yield to the ignorance that permits some men to dominate the unknowing. So Pike's primary lesson calls to mind the old IBM slogan that used to appear in every workplace: the simple advice, "THINK!" That very concept is offensive to many a fundamentalist evangelist, who will happily do all the thinking his followers will ever need.

Some of the critics of Masonry cite the degree work, but more find their raw material for Masonic condemnation in Pike's writings, especially his ponderous *Morals and Dogma*, an 861-page volume that many Masons own, but few have read. It is not only tedious reading, but is full of Pike's own perceptions of Masonry. Many Masons will agree with some statements, but there are others that no Mason will ever believe. Pike was so wrapped up in his knowledge of ancient faiths and philosphic systems that he tended to make the background of Masonry far more complex and esoteric than it was ever meant to be. In some of his chapters, if the words "Mason" and "Masonry" were removed, it is reasonable to believe that many a Mason reading it would not recognize his own fraternity.

Pike was a man with an extraordinary breadth of knowledge, and it is only natural that he wanted to share it all. Unfortunately, he had just one outlet that he could count on, and he appears to have wanted to find a place for everything he knew in the Southern Jurisdiction of Scottish Rite. The teachings of Masonry are simple and clear. Pike preferred them to be festooned with mystic interpretations and deep, arcane meanings.

Make no mistake: Pike was a dynamic force in establishing a strong membership in his own jurisdiction, and a strong force in establishing degree work that has lasted for a hundred years. He was a towering figure in the history of American Masonry. What he was *not* was a Grand Master of any Grand Lodge, who alone is the final authority in basic Masonic practices and jurisprudence. He was never a spokesman for all of Freemasonry and never tried to assert himself as such. He was a strong man who never shrank from expressing his personal opinions, and it is important to remember that his pronouncements as they relate to Masonry are just that: his own opinions.

That's why the most important part of *Morals and Dogma* may be its preface. Not written by Pike himself, the preface was, and is, the official statement of The Supreme Council, the governing body of Scottish Rite Masonry that published his work. It has been ratified by every succeeding Supreme Council, up to this very day. In part, it says (italics mine):

> In preparing this work, the Grand Commander [Pike] has been about equally Author and Compiler; since he has extracted quite half its contents from the works of the best writers and most philosophic or eloquent thinkers. *Perhaps it would have been better and more acceptable if he had extracted more and written less.*

To remove any thought that the work contains religious dogma for Scottish Rite Masons, the preface says:

> The teachings of these readings are not sacramental, so far as they go beyond the realm of Morality into those other domains of Thought and Truth. The ancient and accepted Scottish Rite uses the word "Dogma" in its true sense, of *doctrine*, or *teaching*; and is not *dogmatic* in the odious sense of that term.

And now the most important sentence in the preface (and, once again, the italics are mine):

> *Everyone is entirely free to reject and dissent from*
> *whatsoever herein may seem to him to be untrue or*
> *unsound.*

I was very relieved to find that statement at the beginning of *Morals and Dogma*, because there is much in it that I "reject and dissent from." Such a statement requires at least one example, and I offer the following quote from page 819:

"The Blue Degrees [first, second and third] are but the outer court ᴏᴿ portico of the Temple. Part of the symbols are displayed there to the Initiate, but he is intentionally misled by false interpretations. It is not intended that he shall understand them; but it is intended that he shall imagine that he understands them. Their true explication is reserved for the Adepts, the Princes of Masonry (the 28th degree and beyond)." I have asked enough Masons to convince myself that there is no Mason anywhere who agrees with that statement.

His historical facts are usually correct, but that cannot always be said of his opinions. As an historian who has spent years researching the history of the crusading order of the Knights Templar, I was appalled to read Pike's words, "The Templars were unintelligent and therefore unsuccessful Jesuits," and "Their watchword was to become wealthy, in order to buy the world."

On the other hand, most Christians will agree with much of what Albert Pike has to say about his own faith in Christianity. His discussion of baptism calls the Christian rite "a baptism of repentance, for the remission of sins: that is, the necessity of repentance proven by *reformation*." That "reformation" of the repentant baptized Christian is now being referred to as being "born again," which puts Pike's definition of the sacrament right in line with the beliefs of those who condemn him most angrily. His critics, of course, never quote those points: Their aim is to extract comments about the many religions, sects, and cults described in *Morals and Dogma*, so that they can be cited, regardless of their original content, as "documentation" that Masons believe the teachings of those ancient cults, and *must* believe them. They know they are lying, but quoting out of context is too wonderful a tool to be abandoned.

Nothing thrills the anti-Mason as much as Pike's references to Lucifer. Most Christians reading this will immediately recognize Lucifer as the fallen angel, as Satan, the ruler of hell. Why then, does Pike express his surprise in the words "*Lucifer, the light-bearer!* Strange and mysterious name to give to the Spirit of Darkness! Lucifer, the Son of the Morning! Is it *he* who bears the *Light*, and with its intolerable light blinds feeble, sensual or selfish souls?" He is upset, referring at one point to "the false Lucifer of the legend." What false legend?

I set out to learn for myself, and what I learned may upset many Christians, who have to be told that the King James version of the Bible, which they revere as the literal, precise, correct work of God, is not always so. Some of the error in it was quite deliberate, including the biblical designation of Lucifer as Satan, along with the concordant story of a fallen angel. It is difficult to anticipate the reactions of some believers on being told that there are gross mistakes in the King James version, but, please, do not throw this book across the room in disgust until you have read a bit more.

Lucifer makes his appearance in the fourteenth chapter of the Old Testament book of Isaiah, at the twelfth verse, and nowhere else: "How art thou fallen from heaven, O Lucifer, son of the morning! How art thou cut down to the ground, which didst weaken the nations!"

The first problem is that Lucifer is a Latin name. So how did it find its way into a Hebrew manuscript, written before there was a Roman language? To find the answer, I consulted a scholar at the library of the Hebrew Union College in Cincinnati. What Hebrew name, I asked, was Satan given in this chapter of Isaiah, which describes the angel who fell to become the ruler of hell?

The answer was a surprise. In the original Hebrew text, the fourteenth chapter of Isaiah is not about a fallen angel, but about a fallen Babylonian king, who during his lifetime had persecuted the children of Israel. It contains no mention of Satan, either by name or reference. The Hebrew scholar could only speculate that some early Christian scribes, writing in the Latin tongue used by the Church, had decided for themselves that *they* wanted the story to be about a fallen angel, a creature not even mentioned in the original Hebrew text, and to whom *they* gave the name "Lucifer."

Why Lucifer? In Roman astronomy, Lucifer was the name given to the morning star (the star we now know by another Roman name, Venus). The morning star appears in the heavens just before dawn, heralding the rising sun. The name derives from the Latin term *lucem ferre*, "bringer, or bearer, of light." In the Hebrew text the expression used to describe the Babylonian king before his death is *Helal*, son of *Shahar*, which can best be translated as "Day star, son of the Dawn." The name evokes the golden glitter of a proud king's dress and court (much as his personal splendor earned for King Louis XIV of France the appellation, "The Sun King").

The scholars authorized by the militantly Catholic King James II to translate the Bible into current English did not use the original Hebrew texts, but used versions translated from the Catholic Vulgate Bible produced largely by St. Jerome in the fourth century. It was replete with inaccuracies that included this mistranslation of a Hebraic metaphor describing the downfall of a mighty secular oppressor. Jerome called him Lucifer, and made the king a disobedient angel consigned to rule in hell for all eternity. A great body of Christian mythology has built up over the centuries, based on nothing more than what was probably an erroneous translation into Latin of the Old Testament text in Hebrew.

So "Lucifer" is nothing more than an ancient Latin name for the morning star, the bringer of light. That can be confusing for Christians who identify Christ himself as the morning star, a term used as a central theme in many Christian sermons. Jesus refers to himself as the morning star in Revelation 22:16: "I Jesus have sent mine angel to testify unto you these things in the churches. I am the root and the offspring of David, and the bright and morning star."

And so there are those who do not ready beyond the King James version of the Bible, who say "Lucifer is Satan: so says the Word of God," while others with knowledge of the Latin and Hebrew texts say, "No, Lucifer is the classical Roman name for the morning star, and now Jesus is the morning star." This discussion can only anger certain fundamentalists. (I have at hand an evangelical tract from a Baptist church that says, "I believe in the Infallibility and Preservation of God's Word, of which the King James 1611 authorized version is the God-guided faithful translation.")

Fortunately, this issue of errors in biblical translations is not one that we have to struggle with ourselves. Generations of biblical scholars of all faiths have been aware of the mistranslations and of the misunderstandings that arise from the use of archaic terms whose meanings have been lost, or have evolved into different usages. To address these problems a conference was held in October 1946, attended by delegates of the Church of England, the Church of Scotland, and the Baptists, Methodists, and Congregationalist churches. At another meeting four months later, delegates from the Presbyterians and Quakers joined the original group, along with representatives of various Bible societies. Still later, observers were sent as representatives of the Roman Catholic Church.

The work on a new translation of the Bible, direct from the sources, stretched out over several years. The most distinguished biblical scholars and specialists in the world were invited to contribute, and every delegate was given the opportunity to review and express his own views on every verse, every word, as presented by the translators.

The result of this prodigious joint effort was *The New English Bible*, of which the New Testament was published in 1969 and the Old Testament one year later.

That does not mean that I have cast aside my King James version: I have them both. But I must recognize that while God may be the inspirational source of all the Old and New Testament scriptures, He is certainly not responsible for the imperfect translations from the language of the earliest surviving texts. To err is human, and men can become overzealous because of the emotional aspects of the subject.

To the point, the verse in the King James version (Isaiah 14:12) that begins "How art thou fallen from heaven, O Lucifer . . ." has now been translated directly from the Hebrew in the New English Bible as "How you have fallen from heaven, bright morning star . . ." There is no mention of Lucifer, no reference to any disobedient angel plunging to hell, nor should there be.

The emphasis here should be on *intent*. When Albert Pike and other Masonic scholars spoke over a century ago about the "Luciferian path," or the "energies of Lucifer," they were referring to the morning star, the light bearer, the search for light; the very antithesis of dark, satanic evil.

Still, I believe that Pike was wrong to use Lucifer in the scholarly sense. I remember an old man saying to me years ago, on a different subject, "It may be correct, but it just ain't right!" He had an excellent point. To be "correct" may be good for scholars writing for the enlightenment of other scholars: but for those with a real desire to communicate, recognition must be given to the common usage of words and terms. To this day some learned writers, as did Pike, have difficulty concentrating on *communication*, which may require explaining their terms of reference and curbing their vocabularial excess. To engage in the arrant pedantry of egregious sesquipedalianism (as in this sentence) is not communication. It's showing off. Pike must have known that virtually every Christian of this time firmly believed that Lucifer was Satan. He should have explained his use of the name, or he should have avoided it. And he should have held his scholarly vocabulary in check. However impressive the command of a language a writer may possess, if it cannot be understood as intended and baffles the reader, it is failing in its primary purpose, which should be clear, understandable communication.

Unfortunately, even if Albert Pike had refined his cumbersome style, or reduced the overwhelming variety of information he offered in his works, he would still be the target of vitriolic abuse. The reason is a proved and blatant forgery that is brandished to the great joy and delight of almost every anti-Masonic writer and speaker.

It all began in the late nineteenth century with a man who would do anything, say anything, or write anything to further his own career, untroubled by conscience or morality. His pen name was Léo Taxil. To fully understand the source of much of today's most bitter anti-Masonry, it is necessary to drop back about a hundred years and examine the career of this strange man who, to serve his own ends, maliciously draped the mantle of Lucifer as Satan on the memory of Albert Pike.

6

The Forger

H IS REAL NAME was Gabriel Jogang Pagés, born in the south of France in 1854. His parents arranged for his schooling by the Jesuits, and could only have been proud of his outstanding academic record.

Although well trained, Gabriel chose not to follow a religious career after finishing his education, for that would have entailed abandoning the worldly goods he craved so much. Nor was he inclined to achieve wealth through the time-consuming method of hard work and thrift. He tried the shortcut of financial fraud, and when he was discovered he fled from France to Switzerland. There, Gabriel Pagés adopted the name of Léo Taxil.

He could have change his name but not his character, and his involvement in yet another fraudulent financial scheme led to his ejection from Switzerland. Ever resourceful, Taxil contrived to return to his native France under an amnesty arrangement in 1879, and, once settled, he decided to enter the publishing trade. He was a prolific writer, and a good one. He was willing to put pen to paper on any subject and even tried his hand at pornography, abandoning it only when it failed to show a profit.

As he considered possible markets for his talents, Léo Taxil decided to fan the flames of the anti-Catholic fever sweeping Europe in those years of turbulent political unrest. In an attempt to bolster the Church's spiritual authority in the face of a mounting assault on its secular power, Pope Pius IX had called a Vatican council in 1870. Many Catholics were shocked and disconcerted by the council's proclamation of papal infallibility: When the pope spoke *ex cathedra*, "from the throne" of St. Peter, on matters of faith or morals, he was now incapable of error. This went beyond any claim made by even the most power-driven popes who had preceded Pius IX, and led many of the faithful to leave the Church. Others had disagreed with the same pope's 1854 revelation of the dogma of the Immaculate Conception of the Virgin Mary, claiming that Jesus' mother had been conceived without original sin, through the special grace of God. The dissenters felt that the dogma elevated Mary to a spiritual position equal to Christ himself, which had no basis in New Testament scripture.

Aside from the religious turmoil, Pius IX had to struggle with grave secular problems. The biggest of these were the revolutions mounted against the corruption within the church government in the Papal States. The ambassadors of France, Austria, Russia, and Prussia joined together to deliver a memorandum urging Pius IX to institute democratic reforms and establish nonecclesiastical financial controls. The Holy See was adamant; it would surrender none of its autocratic authority. Revolts erupted in Sicily and in Italy, causing France to send troops to Rome to support the papacy, against strong opposition from a large body of the French people. The Sicilians, led by Giuseppe Garibaldi, rallied in support of a unified kingdom of Italy under King Victor Emmanuel II. When the papal army was defeated the Papal States were occupied, except for the city of Rome.

France sent troops to keep the revolutionaries out of Rome itself, but at the outbreak of the Franco-Prussian war, the French forces were withdrawn to fight in their own war, and the revolutionaries marched into Rome. A plebiscite was held for the Roman citizens who had been prevented by the French occupation from voting for or against Italian unification. As it had in the Papal States, the vote in Rome revealed overwhelming opposition to papal control.

In 1870, for the first time in centuries, the Vicar of Christ held only the title of Supreme Pontiff of the Roman Catholic Church, and would never again rule as a worldly king.

In the strongly anti-Church climate existing throughout France, Léo Taxil believed that he would find a ready market for anticlerical publications. He wrote anti-Catholic satires, poked fun at church leaders, and even revived the ancient myth of "Pope Joan." The story, with no documentation to back it, was that a woman in the church hierarchy had concealed her sex so cleverly that she had succeeded in being elected pope. She was allegedly discovered only when she fell to the street in a swoon during the course of a papal parade to the Lateran palace, and proceeded to give birth to a child.

In hopes of gathering anti-Church material, Taxil joined a lodge of Freemasons in Paris in 1881. His true character quickly surfaced, and he was expelled from the lodge before going beyond the first degree.

Over the succeeding years, his anti-Catholic writing brought him very little income but earned him a great deal of criticism and condemnation from the clergy. He needed another target for his literary talents. That new direction came through what appeared to Taxil to be divine intervention, in the form of an 1884 encyclical, promulgated by the successor of Pius IX, who had taken the papal name of Leo XIII. In all the history of the conflict between the Roman Church and the Masonic order, the encyclical *Humanum Genus* was the most bitter and detailed condemnation of Freemasonry ever written.

This document expressed Pope Leo's frustration, as described earlier. This had been a century of devastating material losses for the Holy See. Plantations, mines, real estate, and millions of acres of rich land in Mexico and South America from which streams of silver and gold had flowed to Rome had been lost to revolutions. And now even the Papal States were gone, and the pope was no more than the bishop of Rome in a state that his predecessors had ruled as autocratic monarchs.

What was most frustrating was that papal rule had been rejected by a *vote*. The people had forgotten, or ignored, the fact that rulers were not selected by an election, but by the will of God. No monarch in Europe took power until crowned and anointed by an official of the Church. *Vox populi*, the voice of the people, had nothing to do with the process. Who were these revolutionaries who could so blatantly defy the will of God and the Vicar of Christ on earth? What motivated them?

As we have seen, the pope's advisors were able to answer that question: They were all Freemasons. Freemasonry therefore must be the source of the revolutionaries' warped sense of government, and the Catholic world must be warned to abhor and avoid this evil organization. The result was *Humanum Genus*.

In the encyclical, Leo XIII did not specifically cite devil worship among Masons, but he branded every non-Catholic in the world a member of the kingdom of Satan and wrote that they "seem to conspire and strive all together under the guidance and with the help of that society of men spread all over, and solidly established, which they call Free-Masons."

And of what crimes were these Masons guilty? Belief in freedom of religion, for one thing—but let the pope tell us in his own words:

> By opening their gates to every creed they promote, in fact, the great modern error of religious indifference and the parity of all worships, the best way to annihilate every religion, especially the Catholic Church, which, being the only true one cannot be joined with others without enormous injustice.

Leo XIII was especially offended that Masons were teaching democratic ideals:

> . . . that men all have the same rights, and are perfectly equal in condition; that every man is naturally independent . . . that it is tyranny to keep men subject to any other authority than that which emanates from themselves. Hence, the people are sovereign; those who rule have no authority but by the commission and concession of the people; so that they can be deposed, willing or unwilling, according to the wishes

of the people. The origin of all rights and civil duties is in the people or in the State, which is ruled according to the new principles of liberty.

(It is perplexing to realize that the pope in 1884 was condemning all of the foregoing as *satanic*.)

The key point that spelled opportunity for Léo Taxil appeared at the end of *Humanum Genus*. The pope called upon all Catholic bishops to teach all the people, and especially the children, the evils of Freemasonry, and its democratic leanings:

> Insist that parents and spiritual directors, in teaching the catechism, may never cease to admonish appropriately children and pupils of the wicked nature of these sects, that they may also learn in time the various fraudulent arts which their propagators use to entice. Those who prepare children for first communion will do well if they will persuade them to promise not to give their names to any society without asking their parents' or their pastor's or their confessor's advice.

Pope Leo had a plan for the bishops:

> We entreat and pray you, venerable brethren, who co-operate with us, to root out this poison, which spreads widely throughout the Nations . . . the first thing to do is to strip from the Masonic sect its mask and show it as it is, teaching orally and by pastoral letters the people about the frauds used by these societies to flatter and entice, the perversity of its doctrines, and the dishonesty of its works.

Here was Taxil's market, the chance to make some real money! The pope had exhorted the bishops to preach and teach against Freemasonry, but he hadn't given them much to go on, other than the Masonic dedication to the principles of democracy. He had said that the Masons were part of the Kingdom of Satan, but he had said that about all non-Catholics. What Léo Taxil could produce was a wealth of anti-Masonic material to use in following the pope's orders. He didn't know much more about Masonry than did the pope himself, but Taxil had never let ignorance of the facts stand in his way; he simple made up whatever would suit his needs. He now set out to provide "facts" that would specifically identify Freemasons as worshippers of Satan.

To capture the right spirit before launching into his new campaign, Léo Taxil confessed to the sins he had committed in writing and publishing anti-Catholic pamphlets. He then undertook the prescribed penance and further emphasized his desire to become a good Catholic again by going off on a meditational retreat. Having thus demonstrated his restoration to a state of grace, Taxil returned home fired up with his newly adopted anti-Masonic zeal and exploded into a frenzy of writing. One book after another appeared, each condemning the Freemasons. The titles are revealing: *The Anti-Christ and the Origin of Masonry; The Cult of the Great Architect;* and *The Masonic Assassins*, to name just a few.

What Taxil lacked was any specific documentation: He needed a shocking revelation to back his allegations, so that the world would recognize his self-appointed role as the most knowledgeable anti-Mason in the world. To be the author of that counterfeit document, he chose Albert Pike. Pike had been dead for several years, so Taxil could expect that his fraud would be safe from exposure and rebuttal. The Southern Jurisdiction of Scottish Rite, which Albert Pike had headed, called its governing board "The Supreme Mother Council of the World." Taxil was fully aware that the title referred only to the Southern Scottish Rite, but the grandiose terminology was easy to twist so that Taxil could present it to his Catholic audience as the Supreme Council of worldwide Freemasonry, with Albert Pike as the ruler of the entire fraternity.

Léo Taxil needed a clear, incontrovertible statement to be used in his forged document so that its significance would be easily and universally recognized. That statement was finally honed to the simple declaration "Lucifer is God," which Taxil would attribute to Albert Pike. The complete forged document follows – but first, a brief explanation of the term "Adonay," which appears in the text.

The ancient Hebrews were reluctant to even whisper the ineffable name of God, expressed in the told texts as JHVH, since written Hebrew has no vowels. Although there can be no certainty about the pronunciation of these letters, known to scholars as the tetragrammation, they are usually converted to *Yahweh*. Rather than say out loud that sacred name, Jews refer to God by a designation of supreme reverence, roughly equivalent to "The Lord," which is *Adonai*. In the course of time, Christians converted *Yahweh* to Jehovah, while the Catholic liturgy used *Adonai* to refer to the second member of the Holy Trinity, who is Jesus Christ. Since Taxil was writing as a Catholic author for a Catholic readership, he uses "Adonay" in this document as a reference to Jesus. What follows was falsely identified as part of a speech and written order which Albert Pike was supposed to have delivered to Freemasons in Paris on Bastille Day, July 14, 1889:

> That which we must say to the world is that we worship a god, but it is the god that one adores without superstition. To you, Sovereign Grand Inspectors General, we say this, that you may repeat it to the brethren of the 32nd, 31st and 30th degrees: The Masonic Religion should be, by all of us initiates of the higher degrees, maintained in the Purity of the Luciferian doctrine. If Lucifer were not God, would Adonay and his priests calumniate him?"
>
> Yes, Lucifer is God, and unfortunately Adonay is also god. For the eternal law is that there is no light without shade, no beauty without ugliness, no white without black, for the absolute can only exist as two gods; darkness being necessary for light to serve as its foil as the pedestal is necessary to the statue, and the brake to the locomotive.
>
> Thus, the doctrine of Satanism is a heresy, and the true and pure philosophical religion is the belief in Lucifer, the equal of Adonay; but Lucifer, God of Light and God of Good, is struggling for humanity against Adonay, the God of Darkness and Evil.

Pike had been dead for three years, so Taxil back-dated the order. It was signed by Taxil as the work of "Albert Pike, Sovereign Pontiff of Universal Freemasonry, Instructions to the twenty-three Supreme Councils of the World, July 14, 1889."

No one in Freemasonry ever held the title of "Sovereign Pontiff." The word pontiff comes from the Latin *pontifex*, and *pontifex* derives from two Latin words, *pons*, meaning "bridge" and *facere*, meaning "to make." The *pontifex* of ancient Rome was a high priest considered to be a "bridge" between the people and the gods. Up to fifteen *pontifices* ruled on all religious matters in the city of Rome, and their leader was called the *Pontifex Maximus*, the Supreme High Priest. Much later, it pleased the popes in Rome to claim for themselves this Latin title from the pre-Christian era, which translates as Supreme Pontiff in English. In tacking the title "Sovereign Pontiff" to Albert Pike's name, Taxil knew full well that his Christian readers in France would presume that Pike must be the satanic rival to the Holy Father in Rome.

Also, the phrase "Universal Freemasonry" has never been used, since there is no such thing. Of the hundreds of Masonic bodies in the world at that time, Pike was the leader of just one, the Southern Jurisdiction of the Scottish Rite.

In spite of its blatant fraudulence, Taxil's forgery was a huge success. The Church was so gratified by his anti-Masonic endeavors that he was honored with a private audience with the pope, who encouraged Taxil to continue in his good work, completely unaware of the cynical hoax being foisted on the whole Catholic world by this man he praised.

The money poured in, as Léo Taxil learned what many hate-mongers today have learned and benefited from: He did not have to live only on the sale of his books and pamphlets. He could part the faithful from their money for contributions to his "ministry," which they were assured would earn them God's favor.

Once in possession of all the wealth he needed, the bogus evangelist was so overwhelmingly proud of his fraudulent achievements that he reached the point where he could no longer keep his triumph to himself. On April 19, 1897, Taxil used his celebrity status to attract a large audience to a meeting in Paris. Journalists came, along with members of the Catholic hierarchy. As Taxil rose to speak, his audience waited in eager anticipation, expecting to hear the latest "revelations" about the satanic Freemasons. Instead, an exuberant Léo Taxil stunned them as he gleefully bragged that for the past twelve years he had fooled them all. He laughed at them for swallowing like innocent babes the drivel that he had created to amass a tidy fortune for himself. Every word written about Masonic devil worship was the product of his own fertile imagination, and they had bought it—literally.

The uproar caused by his boastful confession to his furious and indignant listeners forced Taxil to seek police protection, which became even more necessary when a Paris newspaper published the thirty-three page text of his speech the following week.

Having achieved his financial goal, Léo Taxil had apparently timed his confession to coincide with his plans for retirement. The incorrigible opportunist moved away from Paris to a stately home in the country, where he enjoyed a comfortable life until his death at the age of fifty-three, in 1907.

Taxil's hoax lived on, in spite of the truth being made known, because he had become the richest source of anti-Masonic "documentation" for the hate-mongers. Much of his slanderous output, including the Albert Pike forgery, had been picked up by other secular and religious authors *before* his confession, and was printed as absolute truth. The work of those authors is quoted by subsequent anti-Masonic writers, perfectly willing to keep the lies alive.

Even today, writers determined to prove the existence of devil worship in the Masonic lodge triumphantly present the Pike forgery, even when they know the truth of its history. The statement "Lucifer is God" is just too wonderfully damning to cast aside, false as it is.

The problem is, of course, that whether false statements are published through a vitriolic dedication to destroying Freemasonry, or through simple ignorance of the truth, there are those who read those statements and believe them. An example of this is the use of this same Pike forgery in a recent book by Pat Robertson. Mr. Robertson's book had been out only a few weeks when an angry Christian took the quotation from the book and sent it to the *Tennessee*

7

The Media Mogul

P AT ROBERTSON IS a genuine millionaire media mogul. He is constantly in pursuit of more power and influence, which manifested itself when he made an unsuccessful pass at becoming president of the United States in 1988.

In 1991 Mr. Robertson published an anti-Masonic book titled *The New World Order*. It may be considered potentially more damaging than most of its kind because the author is something of a celebrity, with his "700 Club" on TV here and abroad, his "Family Channel" on cable television, his Christian Broadcasting Network, Untied States Media Corporation, and "Operation Blessing." Pat Robertson's ambitions are kept alive by his newspaper, the *Christian-American*, coupled with his political organization, The Christian Coalition.

Robertson claims for himself all the Christian virtues except, apparently, humility. In his anti-Masonic book he write, ". . . some readers might wish to say to me: Pat, you are an Anglo-Saxon and an Ivy League law graduate. Your father was a Senior United States Senator and you have a distinguished heritage that goes from colonial days back to the nobility of England. You qualify to play a leadership role in the Establishment and its plans for a new world order." His ancestors in the great Clan Robertson might be proud of the financial success of one of their progeny, but probably would not be too happy to find themselves labeled "Anglo-Saxon" and part of the English nobility. And the many Freemasons might wonder why he failed to mention that his father, the senior senator, was also a dedicated Mason.

Robertson's book "exposes" a great international plot to take over the world, destroy government, and wipe out Christianity. There are several villains involved, including the United Nations and the U.S. Federal Reserve Bank. Robertson, however, seems to take particular delight in revealing that the great conspiracy operates within the higher degrees of the Southern Jurisdiction of Scottish Rite Masonry, his major villains in this evil scheme. The make-believe plot, of course, was not hatched in the upper reaches of Freemasonry, but in the nether regions of Mr. Robertson's own devious mind.

His celebrity status did earn for Pat Robertson a review of his book in the *Wall Street Journal*, a piece headlined "A New World Order Nut." At first I thought that the reviewer was being a bit harsh, but after reading the book, I could see that he had actually been generous.

In the forward to *The New World Order*, Mr. Robertson expresses his gratitude to "all the people who have helped with the research, analysis and information gathering." He thanks two of them by name; a Ph.D. and his network news director. As a writer, I could envy him his access to a team of research professionals, but I was less envious when the quality of their professional efforts became apparent.

One small example of Mr. Robertson's history lessons might help to set the stage for the level of credibility in his Masonic conclusions, even when assisted by a research staff. Anyone with even a superficial knowledge of the history of medieval Europe knows that the Black Death was carried there from Central Asia by *fleas* living on the bodies of ships' rats. Once ashore the fleas quickly spread to household rats, to farm animals (who were often part of the household), and to human beings. *Fleas.* Robertson found it convenient to change history to make a point of his own.

He is describing the failures of world governments to deal with environmental problems. Commenting on the spread of disease by pollution in South America, he writes (italics mine): "In most of these places, people are pouring raw, untreated sewage into the streams and into the oceans, and diseases spread there. *That is precisely how the Black Death started in Europe in the fourteenth century.*"

Some of his followers might say in Robertson's defense, "Well, he may get his history mixed up sometimes, but his sense of *morality* is always right on target." Perhaps. He certainly appears to be morally on target with this: "The eighth commandment, 'You shall not steal,' means that the God of Jacob forbids a citizen to take what belongs to another citizen. He did not permit Robin Hood to take from the rich and give to the poor, or the greedy rich to steal the possessions of the poor." That appears to be a crystal-clear moral position, especially when we find one of the "Principal Beliefs" of his Christian Coalition to be, ". . . in honesty and frugality in the distribution of public funds as a matter of stewardship before God."

But read what Mr. Robertson has to say about the Third World country of Zaire. Commenting on the theft of funds provided to Zaire by other countries, principally the United States, he forgives the stealing (which actually ran to many millions of dollars) with the following astonishing statement: "Who could blame an official with a wretched salary and little business sophistication for occasionally dipping into the torrent of money passing before him?" Does that comment about "little business sophistication" imply that this Ivy League lawyer believes that poverty and ignorance absolve thieves from blame, while morality and God's laws apply only to graduates of business schools? In any case, Mr. Robertson just won't blame the leaders of the brutal African governments for *anything.* He blames all of their sins on their former masters, for granting those countries freedom "too soon," before they were ready for it. Are we allowed to remember countless religious leaders loudly condemning any European leaders who dared to make that assertion during those tumultuous years when colonial Africa was clamoring for independence and the expulsion of the imperial masters?

Of primary interest to us, of course, is the impact of this twisted mental process in Pat Robertson's attacks on Freemasonry, where truth takes an especially brutal beating.

From the hundreds of thousands of words that poured from Albert Pike's pen to describe hundreds of ancient deities, it is not at all difficult to select a passage here and there; present it out of context with either a distorted explanation or none at all; and declare, "See! This is what Freemasons believe!" A single example should do to illustrate the point.

Mr. Robertson presents a seven-word quote from Pike's *Morals and Dogma*, "Everything good in nature comes from Osiris," followed by his own parenthetic explanation, "(the Egyptian sun God; the all-seeing eye is a Masonic representation of Osiris)." That quotation is in fact a tiny part of Pike's lengthy explanation of religious beliefs in ancient Egypt. Pike begins this section with (italics mine), "We have heretofore, in the 24th degree, recited the principal incidents in the *Legend* of Osiris and Isis, and it remains to point out the astronomical phenomena (sun, moon and stars) which it has converted into *mythological* facts." Understandably, Mr. Robertson chooses to leave out the point that the worship of Osiris is presented by Pike to his readers as *legend* and *mythological*, because his intention is to mislead. If he had quoted in full context, his readers would have seen at once that "Every good thing in nature comes from Osiris" was a statement, and a true statement, about what *ancient Egyptians* believed, not what Freemasons believe. To twist the truth like this for the express purpose of blackening other men's reputations is vicious and, in my personal opinion, criminal.

Early in his book, Mr. Robertson finds an ominous warning of the dark conspiracy in the Great Seal of the United States, as reproduced on our one-dollar bill. Mr. Robertson's interpretations of our Great Seal are weird. It's not the weirdness of a babbling idiot, however, but the deliberate word and thought manipulation of a skilled propagandist. And since he has now convinced at least some of his readers that Freemasons worship Osiris, he finds it easy to say that the eye in the Great Seal is not the eye of Divine Providence, the eye of God—which is what it really represents—but is instead the eye of Osiris, the ancient Egyptian god.

Below that eye on the seal is a truncated pyramid that bears the Roman numerals for 1776, the year of the Declaration of Independence. Next, Robertson calls attention to the Latin motto that encircles the pyramid. It reads *Annuit Coeptis* above, and *Novus Ordo Seclorum* below. Latin scholars translate *Annuit Coeptis* as "A time of beginning," a sensible reference to 1776. Robertson translates it as "He looks favorably on our endeavor," with "He looks" apparently referring to the eye of Osiris. *Novus Ordo Seclorum* means "A new order for (coming) generations." Robertson chooses to translate it as "New order of the ages," or "New world order," the title of his book.

The word *seclorum* may be confusing. At the time of the pre-Christian Roman poet Virgil, from whom the second part of the Latin motto is taken, *seculum* meant "generation," and was sometimes used to mean an "age," or a fixed period of time. Much later, the Roman Church decided that the Church alone would exist forever in an unbroken stream. Therefore, it could not be measured in units of genera or time (*tempus*), or in generations (*secula*). Therefore, the Church referred to the nonspiritual world as "secular" or "temporal." Nothing in the motto means "world," for which the Latin word in *mundus*. Robertson's assertion that the motto on the Great Seal of the United States means that Osiris looks with favor on a New World Order is ridiculous, but necessary for him to set the stage for the great Masonic conspiracy.

Having asserted his own creative Latin translation and interpretation, Pat Robertson is troubled by it. "Is it possible," he writes, "that a select few had a plan, revealed in the Great Seal adopted at the founding of the United States, to bring forth, not the nation that our founders and champions of liberty desired, but a totally different world order under a mystery religion designed to replace the old Christian world order of Europe and America?"

If the Masonic leaders at the time of this country's founding were indeed the perpetrators of this abominable scheme, as Mr. Robertson wants us to believe, they should be revealed by name, so that historians can be wary of them. The evil men he is referring to, the Masonic leaders, included George Washington, Benjamin Franklin, James Monroe, Paul Revere, Robert Livingston, John Hancock, Peyton Randolph, Israel Putnam, George Rogers Clark, John Paul Jones, and Nathaniel Greene. Were these the men bent on thwarting the plans of the "founders and champions of liberty"? (Perhaps Robertson's research team had that month off.)

Before putting the subject of the Great Seal to rest, one more item deserves attention. Mr. Robertson exhibits a compulsion to involve Southern Jurisdiction Scottish Rite Masonry in his allegations of conspiracy, because he is then able to draw upon the prolific writings of Albert Pike and his references to the history of world religions. But Scottish Rite Masonry cannot possible be tied in with his theory about a mysterious message concealed within the newly created Great Seal of the United States. Scottish Rite Masonry didn't even exist at that time: The first council of Scottish Rite was not formed until 1801, after the turn of the century. Furthermore, Albert Pike and his literary efforts cannot be cited in connection with any allegations of a Great Seal conspiracy, because he, too, had not yet been born.

Such details cannot be permitted to divert the dedicated anti-Masonic author, a status Robertson earns by playing follow-the-leader and including the famous Taxil forgery of an order from Albert Pike. He doesn't allude to its status as a proven counterfeit, but says that he presents it "without comment."

Not satisfied to merely repeat accusations leveled against Masonry by other anti-Masonic fundamentalists, Mr. Robertson creates a new piece of "evidence" that is his own invention, as unique as it is false. No doubt remembering his lessons at Yale Law School, he doesn't present his revelation as absolute truth, but begins with the careful words, "It is my understanding that . . . ," and continues with the message: "As part of the initiation for the 32nd degree, the candidate is told that Hiram, the builder of Solomon's Temple, was killed by three assassins. The candidate therefore must strike back at those assassins, which are, courtesy of the Illuminati, the government, organized religion and private property."

What motivation is there that would cause an author to present a description of a Masonic degree that is untrue from beginning to end? Not one *phrase* of it is true. Nowhere in all of Freemasonry, in any of its various systems, is there any condemnation of government, organized religion, or private property. Nowhere!

Then, after creating a Masonic degree that no Freemason would ever accept, he goes on to draw further from his limitless knowledge: "This particular ritual is not Egyptian but from the Hung Society of China, based on the cult of Amitabha Buddha. The ceremony, which clearly resembles those of the Egyptian *Book of the Dead*, was apparently copied as well by the Freemasons. It involves not a builder named Hiram, but a group of Buddhist monks, all of whom were slain by three villains, one of whom was the Manchu emperor Khang Hsi."

This allegation is also very creative. The secret Hung Society, known officially in Chinese as *T'in Tei Hui*, or the Society of Heaven and Earth, existed for centuries before the emperor K'ang-hsi, who reigned from 1662 to 1723. It was a militant political society whose battle cry was "Restore the Ming," the dynasty that had been ousted by the Manchu. It was outlawed as criminal by the Manchu emperors, who also fought for an exclusive position for Confucianism, the state religion, by cruel persecution of the Taoists and Buddhists. The Hung Society was originally of the Taoist faith, but began to include Buddhists after the Amida (Amitabha) Buddha revealed a Buddhist heaven, which he called "The Pure Land," a place of peace and plenty.

His doctrine was useful to the Hung, who could now promise their "soldiers" a reward of immortality, a big improvement over the Taoist creed that the rewards and punishments for good and evil were dispensed during a man's lifetime. Always militant, the Hung spread to wherever Chinese migrated; to America, to Singapore, and to Hong Kong. In the latter crown colony they gradually managed to gain control of gambling, prostitution, and smuggling, and are still identified today by one of their triangular symbols, which caused them to become known as the "Triads."

The problem with Pat Robertson's confident conclusion that K'ang-hsi's persecution of Buddhists was turned into ritual by the Hung, and then copied by the Freemasons, is one of time.

The Masonic degree that describes the assassination of Hiram, master builder of Solomon's temple, is the ancient third degree, not the 32nd. Its legend of the death of Hiram Abiff was firmly in place before K'ang-hsi became emperor of China. Chronologically, it just cannot have been copied from some secret Chinese ritual based on the emperor's religious persecutions. Mr. Robertson really ought to check his facts before he uses them to fabricate a conspiracy to rule the world.

He is not the first to allege such a plot. A conspiracy-revealing book titled *Secret Societies and Subversive Movements* is listed in the bibliography for Robertson's *The New World Order*. Written by the British historian Nesta Webster and published in 1924, *Secret Societies* has been more recently published in a book club edition by the Christian Book Club of America. Robertson asserts that Nesta Webster's writings support his theory of a world takeover conspiracy. What he fails to mention is that Nesta Webster was the most bitter and aggressive anti-Semitic writer of her time. Her conspiracy to take over the world was blamed on the Jews, in cooperation with German bankers, not on the Masons, in cooperation with the U.S. Federal Reserve Bank.

In *Secret Societies*, Mrs. Webster writes, "England . . . banished the Jews in 1290, and it was during the three and half centuries they remained in exile that she was known as 'Merrie England.' The fact that their return in force in 1664 was followed by the Great Plague (1665) and the Great Fire of London a year later would not appear to indicate that the Jews necessarily bring good fortune to the land that protects them." Commenting on the Jewish character she writes, ". . . the spirit of fair play which is the essence of the British character is not the characteristic of the Jewish race in general;" and "The increasing number of Jews in positions of authority in England is cause for alarm."

Equally forthright about political systems that she admired, Mrs. Webster expressed her attitude toward the Fascist government that Mussolini had established in Italy in 1922. She stated her opinion very clearly: "*Fascismo* (Fascism) triumphed in Italy, because it was not, as it has been absurdly represented, a reactionary movement, but it was essentially democratic and progressive, because by appealing to the noblest instincts in human nature, to patriotism and self-sacrifice, it rallied all elements in a disorganized and disunited nation around the standard of a common cause."

That declaration, coupled with Mrs. Webster's conclusion that the great conspiracy to rule the world was initiated by a partnership of Jewish and German leaders, causes one to wonder if the English climate in which she worked fogged up her crystal ball from time to time. And how in the world did a work containing so much bigotry and racism become a selection of a *Christian* book club and serve as a reference work to a man who declares himself to be a great worldwide Christian evangelist?

The one appeal that *Secret Societies* would have held for Pat Robertson was that Mrs. Webster included in her world conspiracy theory what she termed "Continental Masonry," alternately referenced as the "Grand Orient of France," and an organization known as the "Bavarian Illuminati." Robertson eagerly pounced on those names to link American Freemasonry to his own theories.

The term "Illuminati" (enlightened ones) has been claimed by numerous intellectuals and religious sects from time to time, but the Bavarian Illuminati cited by Nesta Webster referred to the Order of the Illuminati, a secret society born in the mind of a man named Adam Weishaupt and launched on May 1, 1776, in Bavaria. Weishaupt hated the Catholic Church and especially the Society of Jesus, the Jesuits. His aims, shared in correspondence with his cohorts, were the abolition of organized religion, the downfall of established rules, and the destruction of national boundaries, so that each man would rule himself. A father would not be only the ruler of his own family, subject to no external laws, but would also be its priest. Weishaupt recognized no deity as such, but appeared to hold that nature is God, so there is no need for an organized church. Weishaupt embraced a communistic view of common ownership, and therefore opposed the concepts of capitalism and private property.

Shortly after forming the Illuminati, Weishaupt joined a Masonic lodge in Munich, with the avowed intention of discovering the "secrets" of Freemasonry. He did not advance very far in the fraternity, but he did formulate a plan to spread his philosophies inside Freemasonry. He urged his followers to become Masons, but he advised them to conceal their antireligious feelings and act like devout Christians. They were to spread their views gradually and to try to persuade their lodge brothers to realize that governments were tyrannical and to join them in lamenting the corruption within the Catholic Church.

Weishaupt's plan worked best in France, where anti-Catholic feeling ran deep, and resentment toward the tyrannical Bourbon monarchy simmered and bubbled, soon to boil over into the French

Revolution. The Grand Lodge of France, called the "Grand Orient," was in the forefront of what writers would subsequently refer to as Continental Masonry, and sometimes as Illuminated Freemasonry, to indicate the Illuminati influence.

The essence of that history of the Illuminati and the Grand Orient of France appear in Pat Robertson's book, but *nothing* of the vital events which took place later. In 1785 an Illuminati emissary on a mission from Bavaria to Silesia was struck dead by lightning. When the body was searched for effects that would yield the name of the dead man, dispatches were found indicating beyond doubt the treasonous nature of the order. A government investigation followed and the Order of the Illuminati was outlawed. Membership in it became a serious criminal offense.

The twisted aims of the Illuminati lived on inside the Grand Orient of France, and it is said that these Illuminated Freemasons played leading roles in the French Revolution of 1789. At that time the Grand Orient had about two thousand lodges and one hundred thousand members.

Since each Grand Lodge is completely autonomous and not subject to control by any other Masonic body, other Masons were unaware of what was going on within the leadership circles of the Grand Orient. In 1887, almost a century after the storming of the Bastille, the Grand Orient had been so thoroughly infused with antireligious zealots that it felt emboldened to make a public declaration. The announcement declared that from that day forward the Grand Orient would set aside some of the most basic principles of Freemasonry. Atheists would be welcome in its lodges: No man had to assert his belief in God or immortality. God would no longer be the object of prayers in the lodge. Its new requirement would be "absolute liberty of conscience, including the acceptability of any man's assertion that there is no God."

British Masonry reacted by severing all ties with the Grand Orient of France; the American Grand Lodges followed soon after. Today, no legitimate Masonic body recognizes the Grand Orient, and no visitations are permitted either way. Even the Catholic Church recognized the schism. It condemned Continental Masons and their political and antireligious goals, while specifically excluding other

Masonic Grand Lodges around the world from that condemnation. Nesta Webster, too, acknowledged the need to clarify the issue, referring to ". . . England, Germany and America . . . where Freemasonry is not subversive . . ." However, Pat Robertson, who apparently gleaned his facts on the Illuminati and Illuminated Freemasonry from *Secret Societies*, fails to mention the true facts about the fate of the Illuminati and the Grand Orient and deliberately encourages his readers to believe that the Illuminated Freemasonry to which he refers is, in fact, American Freemasonry.

The tragedy arising from these distortions and omissions is that, in many quarters, Pat Robertson will be believed. His publishers told me that they have already printed fifty thousand hard-bound copies of *The New World Order*. That means that tens of thousands of men and women will be misled by a man whom they believe is dedicated to speaking the truth and obeying the will of God.

When a writer depends upon a research staff, it is impossible to tell whether or not he has actually read for himself all the books in his bibliography. If he did read Nesta Webster's *Secret Societies* for himself, Pat Robertson would certainly have been struck by one line, a quotation from the German historian von Hammer, who said, "It is nothing to the ambitious man what people believe, but it is everything to know how he may turn them for the execution of his projects."

In the middle of his vicious attacks on Masonry, Mr. Robertson cannot keep from preaching his own conscience-free self-righteousness:

"To my mind," he writes, "there is no more monstrous evil than to bring public-spirited, often churchgoing, men into an organization that looks like a fraternal lodge, then deliberately mislead them until they are solid members. Then move them up thirty degrees to the place where they are ready to learn that Satan is the good god waiting to liberate mankind . . ."

I can think of an evil more monstrous than that: To besmirch the character and reputations of "public-spirited, often churchgoing, men" for no other purpose than to achieve the usual Robertson goals of profits and power.

One special aspect of Robertson's *The New World Order* seems to have gone unnoticed. A couple of years before Robertson's book, a book was published by an Arizona author named A. Ralph Epperson. It was based on the same central thesis: a Masonic conspiracy to rule the world. As its "evidence," it cited some of the same writings that Robertson used later. It even discussed the same alleged Masonic symbolism in the design of the Great Seal on the U.S. dollar bill, although Robertson appears to present it as his own original thinking. I'm quite certain that Mr. Robertson, if questioned on these points, would claim that they are simply innocent coincidences, although he might take a deep breath before asserting that stand on Epperson's title, which was *The New World Order*—precisely the same title Robertson used.

If it is any comfort, the Masons are not the only targets of this man's maniacal mind. In 1992, just a few weeks before the voters of Iowa were to consider an amendment for equal rights for women (primarily the same pay as men for doing the same job), Robertson sent a fund-raising letter (does he write any other kind?) to inform his followers in that state of the real truth. He told them that the real agenda of the feminist movement is not equal rights for women, but rather is to convince good women "to leave their husbands, kill their children, destroy capitalism, practice witchcraft and become lesbians."

If Pat Robertson knows that what he writes is flagrant fabrication, he is a decidedly dangerous man. If, on the other hand, he actually *believes* what he writes, then this poor man is in dire need of therapy.

8

Fundamentalist Fury

THE VICTIMS OF attacks like those made by Mr. Robertson are not just those he tears down, but also the people he purports to be serving. Among the Protestant fundamentalists are to be found some of the most devout Christians in the world. Unfortunately, their devotion and dedication make many of them ready targets for those among them whose cravings for power compel them to put their greed before God.

I had an older sister who died from advanced diabetes, and as her executor I had the task of sorting out her personal papers. They revealed a sadness that had come from the healing promises of a television evangelist. She had a leather box of letters which were obviously precious to her, letters that addressed her in such terms as "Dear Beloved of God" and "Dear Beautiful Person." They were easily recognizable as form letters, with a different typewriter used to fill in her name and address and the amount of her latest contribution.

Each letter was in three basic parts. The first short paragraph expressed gratitude for my sister's gift. The next part explained how much God loved her and would help her for sending the money. The third part, of course, was a plea for more, with several suggestions that she should, in effect, strain her resources to send as large a gift as possible.

A dozen or so letters evidenced amounts she had sent totaling $2,200. The sadness was not in the fact that she had spent the money — it was hers to do with as she wished. It lay in the fact that she had for years attended a little neighborhood church a few blocks away. The minister of that church had visited her and prayed with her, but the television preacher had apparently convinced her that he was in much closer communication with God. She didn't suspect that her money had probably gone to provide a luxurious life-style for the evangelist and to help buy more TV time to enable him to raise even more money. The sadness was that her $2,200 would have meant so much more to her own neighborhood church, where it would have been put to a more direct and effective Christian use and would have earned genuine gratitude, along with real prayers, from her friends in her own church.

Some of those evangelistic leaders have discovered an avenue to wealth and power that has been employed by many leaders for centuries: Implant in a group of people a blend of fear and anger, then assure them that you have both the message and the answers; define the enemy and point to the path of success and security. It is effective in leadership by nationality, by race, and by religious denomination. To Hitler, the enemy was the Jews; to the Serbian Eastern Orthodox leaders it is the Muslim Bosnians; to conservatives it is liberals (and vice versa). And so it goes, as races are stirred up against each other, as nations split apart along ethnic lines, and as competition gets fierce among men who claim to be leading their followers to the one true pathway to the throne of God. That competition grew fierce in recent years as Jimmy Swaggart brought down a competitive evangelist, whose son got his revenge by producing photographs that proved the sexual aberrations of Brother Swaggart, who by then had blown the whistle on Jim Bakker. They all forgave themselves and attributed their actions to the influence of Satan, who hates the godly.

That to many fundamentalists the great enemy is Satan is totally understandable in concept, but what gets weird are the satanic manifestations that professional evangelists sometimes assert in order to stay ahead of their competition. In the city where I live, a giant consumer-products company has for generations used as its trademark a stylized drawing of the man in the moon. Then one day a radical fundamentalist decided that three of the curly hairs in the man's beard were really sixes. He triumphantly announced that hidden in the trademark was 666, the Mark of the Beast, as revealed in the Book of Revelation. And it was hidden in the *moon*, itself a symbol with satanic overtones, since it rules over darkness. The campaign began with the condemnation of the trademark and went so far as to call for boycott of the company's products. The insanity was stopped only in the courts.

In Britain, the government stopped using 666 on license plates, since it was credited with so much evil. One fundamentalist defended himself from a charge of murder on the basis that he had been controlled by the satanic demon in his license plate.

There have been many other fundamentalist revelations of satanic influence—for example, the allegation that the popular music style known as "heavy metal" is satanic in origin, and the ridiculous assertion that when recordings of rock-and-roll music are played backward, they reveal direct messages from Satan to the young people listening to those records.

In such an atmosphere, with fanatics looking for satanic influences everywhere, it is not at all surprising that Freemasonry has been included in the witch hunt. Unfortunately, in their fierce determination to "discover" satanic influences and worship and report them to their followers, the hunters don't mind at all if they must avoid the truth, twist the truth, and even yield to blatant lies in order to support their claims. Freemasonry offers a fertile ground for their malicious teachings, because Masons traditionally do not reply to critics. That absence of response is sometimes cited as "proof" that the Masons are guilty as charged.

I have had occasion to debate anti-Masonic fundamentalists and have taken part in call-in shows on self-styled "Christian" radio stations, operated by and for fundamentalists. I have tried to answer the anti-Masonic allegations of fundamentalist ministries and have borne abuse for defending Masonry, which callers have identified as "pagan," "anti-Christian," and "an instrument of the devil." One caller demanded that I be taken off the air, asking the show host, "Don't you know that anyone who speaks favorably of Freemasonry is an agent of Satan?"

The anti-Masonic material generated by these leaders provides, not surprisingly, a steady source of income for them. Pamphlets, books, audiotapes, and even videotapes (in one case a reenactment of the Masonic ceremony of the third degree) are all available at a price. Such publications drive anti-Masonic propaganda into the minds of devout followers, who believe that what they are told by ordained evangelists *must* be so—to the extent that they become upset, and even angry, when they hear the truth.

In the past year or so, anti-Masonic accusations have turned strongly toward the ritual of the Southern Jurisdiction of the Scottish Rite and the writings of Albert Pike, which we have already addressed. Now let's look at allegations brought against the general concept of Freemasonry and against the teachings of the three degrees of the symbolic lodge that make a man a Master Mason—a status enjoyed by every Freemason in this country. These are the condemnations most frequently heard or read:

ALLEGATION: YOU CAN'T HAVE ONE GOD FOR ALL RELIGIONS."

Freemasonry isn't trying to have one God for everyone, but rather is seeking a means by which all men who believe in a monotheistic God can join together. "God" in the Masonic sense refers to God as perceived and worshipped by the individual Mason. No man is asked to alter his beliefs to meet some Masonic standard, and that is entirely appropriate for a fraternal body that has no desire to be a separate religion.

The Masonic approach is much the same as the approach of the U.S. government and the Founding Fathers. The Declaration of Independence justifies the actions of the revolutionaries, who want "the separate and equal station to which the Laws of Nature and of Nature's God entitle them." A century and a half after the new country was established, the Pledge of Allegiance to the flag called for a belief in "one nation under God." This was clearly a reference to God as perceived by each individual citizen, since there was no state religion and no legal definition of one perception of God to the exclusion of all others.

Perhaps "clearly" is too strong a term. In a debate with a fundamentalist, I proposed a hypothetical federal courtroom in which the plaintiff is Christian, the defendant is Muslim, and the presiding judge is Jewish. Every federal court is opened with the words "May God bless the United States of America and this honorable court." Each of the parties in the room is satisfied that his God has been asked to bless the proceedings and the attempt to discover the truth. My question to the evangelist was, "Tell me, which God is the court official asking to bless the court?" His reply was, "The God of Jesus Christ, of course. No other God has a right to be in the United States." So much for freedom of religion.

ALLEGATION: FREEMASONS CALL ALL MEMBERS "BROTHER," BUT SCRIPTURE TEACHES US THAT THERE IS NO BROTHERHOOD EXCEPT IN CHRIST. THAT'S WHY MASONRY IS ANTI-CHRISTIAN.

There is no winning (or losing) this argument, because it depends solely upon the interpretations of the speaker. My own reactions to Jesus Christ speaking of "my brethren" is that he was speaking of all mankind. It had never occurred to me that there were strong restrictions on the message "Inasmuch as ye have done it unto one of the least of these my brethren, ye have done it unto me," especially considering that when the words were said, there were just a handful of men who might be called Christians. Men have argued, written, and pontificated for almost two thousand years on the meanings of each sentence in the New Testament, and it is clear that the argument still goes on. I can only hope that most people will agree that we *must* find a way for all men around the world to live in brotherhood, or we can never have peace and security. Masonry has made a strong contribution to that goal, but in doing so has had to bear the brunt of fiery-eyed attacks that say, "A true Christian cannot ever be in brotherhood with a Muslim, a Jew, a Mormon, a Unitarian, a Christian Scientist, or a Roman Catholic. Jesus forbids it!"

ALLEGATION: Freemasonry promises that good works will earn salvation, which is a lie. Salvation is available only to the man who accepts Jesus Christ as his personal savior, and good works have nothing to do with it.

This strongest and most frequent assertion is wrong on two counts. First, Freemasonry does not offer salvation on any basis. Each man must find that within his own faith, for salvation is the highest personal goal of any religion, and Freemasonry is certainly no religion. What Freemasonry does convey in lodge lectures is that Masonry offers a man the opportunity to engage in the good works which are required from every believer in every moral religion.

"But good works play absolutely no role in salvation," cries the radical fundamentalist. To which I answer that most of the Masons I have met, almost all of whom are Christians, accept a moral code repeatedly defined in the Scripture, a code that requires sympathy, kindness, and charitable good works. They believe that faith in Jesus Christ as the Son of God is all-consuming and that it lives in the mind and heart, not just in the mouth, and so in the deeds as well as words. To live otherwise is to make mockeries of the Sermon on the Mount and the parable of the Good Samaritan and renders the teachings of the Ten Commandments meaningless and unnecessary.

All that is not going to convince a radical fundamentalist of anything, but rather will cause him to search his Bible for quotations, usually taken out of context, to support his position. Since any argument seems to require scriptural citation, I offer these from the Epistle of James (italics mine):

"What doth it profit, my brethren, though a man *say* he hath faith, and *have not works*? Can faith save him?" (2:14)

"Even so *faith, if it hath not works, is dead*." (2:17)

"But wilt thou know, O vain man, that *faith without works is dead*?" (2:30)

"Ye see then how that by works a man is justified, and *not by faith only*." (2:24)

"For as the body without the spirit is dead, so *faith without works is dead also*." (2:26)

And finally, from The First Epistle of John:

"But whoso hath this world's good, and seeth his brother have need, and shutteth up his bowels of compassion from him, how dwelleth the love of God in him? My little children, let us not love in word, neither in tongue; but in *deed* and in truth." (3:17–18)

"He that saith, I know him, and keepeth not his commandments, is a liar, and the truth is not in him." (2:4)

In essence, what Freemasonry tells a new member is that he should attend and support his own house of worship. When the time comes that his faith and his compassionate humanity prompt him to seek the most effective ways to help those in need, he can join in charitable work with his Masonic brothers who are similarly dedicated.

Thus Masonry does not compete with the Mason's own faith, but complements those aspects of his own faith that call for charitable conduct. As to the beneficiaries of those charities, since Masonry is not a religion, it imposes no requirement of religious affiliation upon them. The Shrine hospitals for crippled and burned children, the Knight Templar subsidies for cataract surgery, the Scottish Rite Language Disorders Centers for children, and the Grand Lodge drug abuse programs are open to those of any nationality, race, or religious belief.

That being true, and it is true, many Masons must wonder how they can be the victims of such unreasonable attacks. To put the matter in perspective, Masons should realize that they are not the sole targets of those scathing condemnations.

The Roman Catholic Church bears the brunt of some especially vicious attacks. I have in front of me a six-page folder identified as the work of Tony Alamo, "World Pastor, Evangelist, Author and renowned expert on Catholic cults." Mr. Alamo identifies Pope John Paul II as a former salesman for the I. G. Farben Chemical Company, in which capacity he reportedly sold cyanide gas to the Nazis for use at Auschwitz. The Vatican is called "Satan's Church," and the author claims that it controls the United Nations, which he tells us is also satanic.

In one paragraph the author presents himself as an "intelligent mind," then goes on to prove that he doesn't even come close to meriting that status:

"It taxes the intelligent mind to understand how depraved popes, like John Paul II, have brainwashed so many people throughout the centuries into a zombie-like cult worship of these incredibly false prophets and their gruesome Nazi religion. It is almost impossible to break a thoroughly brainwashed Catholic out of his or her zombie-like stupor of belief that the imbecile pope is God."

The current thrust of anti-Masonic fundamentalists is that the average Mason does not know that hidden in the "upper hierarchy" of Masonry is a secret conclave of leaders who plot to rule the lives not just of Masons, but of all human society. That is an accusation leveled at others, too; Alamo addresses ". . . you Catholics, one-world and united church people who have no knowledge of the hierarchy wherein you worship." And it should not be overlooked that the source always cited to back up the bigotry and to legitimize the lies is the loving, forgiving, peace-seeking teachings of Jesus Christ, reinforced by out-of-context interpretations of quotations from both the Old and New Testaments.

These are people to worry about, because they don't keep their doctrines of divisiveness and hatred to themselves but feel called upon to shout out their messages on radio, on TV, and in published material, raising money and raising hell to such a high degree that we must reach the depressing conclusion that many people believe that the garbage thrown at them holds some great truth. Freedom of religion and freedom of speech must be preserved at any cost, but the right of free speech does not include the right to lie and to distort the truth.

Some may feel that I have overreacted, but in this situation I'm not certain that it is possible to overreact. It would be tedious to address every piece of anti-Masonic drivel that hits the streets, but taking a detailed look at one of them may help to make the point. It is so trashy that describing it is almost an embarrassment.

It is a little three-by-five-inch cartoon booklet titled *The Curse of Baphomet*. Copies were being handed out on the street in front of the headquarters hotel of the 1991 Conference of Masonic Grand Masters, and I've been shown copies picked up in many other parts of the country. Since any Freemason, his family, or his friends may be taken to task based on this booklet, it appears necessary to examine it in some detail.

The story begins as a policeman appears at the door of the home of a middle-aged couple, to tell them that their son has attempted suicide: His life is hanging in the balance in a hospital intensive-care unit. The doctor observes that the boy *could* make it, but he has no will to live.

A few days later a friend calls to find the parents still despondent, unable to understand what has happened in their family. The father says to the visiting friend, "We're good people, Ed. I'm a church deacon and a good lodge member."

The visitor is horrified. "A lodge member? Alex, are *you* a Mason? . . . I had no *idea* you were into witchcraft." After a brief argument the friend says, "I was a Mason until I found out about *BAPHOMET* . . . This Great Architect of the Universe you pray to is NOT the God of the Bible . . . it's really Baphomet! And he's ugly, frightening and completely satanic."

Masons, who have never heard of Baphomet, will say, "I don't know what the author is talking about," but that's all right: The author doesn't know what he's talking about, either.

When the Knights Templar were arrested back in 1307, they were tortured by the Inquisition to force them into confessions of heresy. Tortured men usually confess what they are told to confess. Of all those men tortured, just *two* confessed that the Templars had an idol, a bearded head called *Baphomet*. There were no details, so some historians speculated that the bearded head was Jesus (remember the Shroud of Turin?). The authors of *Holy Blood, Holy Grail* decided that Baphomet was a corruption of an Arabic term meaning "father of wisdom." English historian Edith Simon wrote that Baphomet was clearly a distortion of the name *Muhammed*. That's it. That's all there is: Baphomet is mentioned in their confessions by two tortured Knights Templar almost seven hundred years ago. There is no other use of Baphomet in all of history or anywhere in Scripture and certainly no place for it in Freemasonry.

Back to the comic book: When the friend produces a picture of Baphomet, it turns out to be a winged creature with the body of a man, the breasts of a woman, and the head of a horned goat. On the forehead is a pentagram (the outline of a five-pointed star). In reference to the star, the ex-Mason friend says to the mother, "Sally, the Eastern Star symbol is an upside-down star, right? Well, it's a satanic symbol." He points out a goat head in the "upside-down star."

Fundamentalist writers (and even a Masonic writer in the nineteenth century) frequently assert that if the single point of a five-pointed star is directed upward, it points to heaven and is a divine symbol. If the single point is downward, it is a satanic symbol, pointing to hell. What they miss is that the Eastern Star is the Star of Bethlehem that guided the three wise men from the east to the birthplace of Jesus. It is pointing down not to hell, but to a stable. (The five-pointed stars on the foreheads of the devil-figure in the booklet, and on its front cover, are pointing *up*, which by the author's definition is godly, not satanic. I'm not going to try to figure out that one.)

Now the ex-Mason visitor points out that Baphomet is also the triple-barred cross used in the 33rd degree of Scottish Rite (an angled form of the Jerusalem Cross). There is a photograph of Henry C. Clausen, Past Sovereign Grand Commander of the Southern Jurisdiction of Scottish Rite, with that cross on his 33rd degree cap. (The fact that a triple-barred cross is also the personal symbol of the pope wouldn't bother most fundamentalist evangelists. They'd happily conclude that he is a devil worshipper, too.)

Then there is a photo of Albert Pike with that cross on a chain. The visiting friend explains in the booklet that Albert Pike is the "Grand Commander Sovereign Pontiff of Universal Freemasonry." Just reading that title tells us what is coming next: the proven forgery of Léo Taxil, which is used over and over again to assert Masonic devil worship.

Next the reader of this tragic comic book is treated to an "explanation" of symbols. A drawing of the Washington Monument is used to illustrate the message, "The obelisk is a Masonic symbol of a male sex organ right out of Baal worship." The all-seeing eye, used as a symbol to remind Masons that God sees all of us and all of our actions, is common to Christianity (as in "His eye is on the sparrow"), but is identified here as being from the Egyptian god Osiris. And Freemasons are bashed for seeking "light," which to almost all the world is synonymous with "knowledge." To the rabid fundamentalist author of the comic book, a Mason seeking light is calling Jesus a liar. (I cannot explain this conclusion, because I fail to understand the reasoning or the religious purpose in rejecting the search for knowledge.)

Now we come to the Shrine, which does not escape condemnation. The dear friend explains that the Shriner's fez in a shrine to Allah. He explains:

"In the 8th century, Muslim hords [sic] overran the Moroccan city of Fez and butchered fifty thousand Christians. The streets ran red with blood. The Muslim murderers dipped their caps in the blood in honor of Allah. These blood-stained caps were called fezzes, idols dedicated to a false god [Satan]."

To begin with, there was no city of Fez until the very end of the eighth century, when it was founded by an invader, Sultan Idris I. Idris took the territory by winning a war against resident pagans, including Berber tribesmen, all of whom were converted to Islam. If any Christians were in the area, history doesn't remember them. As far as the cap is concerned, its manufacture was begun after the second sultan, Idris II, expanded the town to the other side of the river and encouraged local craft industries. The Moroccans had several good dyes, whose formulations were kept secret. One of the dyes was a brilliant red, and until well into the eighteenth century no other place turned out that brilliant red cap. It was in great demand and was named after Fez, the city of its manufacture. It's not a "shrine" to anything—it's a hat.

(The author and publishers of this little booklet could be in deep trouble in other parts of the world, where asserting that Allah is Satan could be life-threatening.) The book sums up Shrinedom with the information that every Shriner swears a "Muslim" oath on the Koran. On the contrary, the altar at the Shrine temple holds the holy books of Christianity, Judaism, and Islam. The Shriner uses the book applicable to his own faith.

Finally, the visiting friend advises the parents, "Renounce Masonry, burn those objects and repent before God . . . so he can remove this curse you have brought on your family." Next, the couple kneel in their backyard by a fire consuming his Masonic regalia, while the father says, "Dear Father, we never knew that Masonry was witchcraft." And then, of course, they get a phone call telling them their son is awake and his depression is gone, because the curse of Masonic witchcraft has been purged from their home.

The booklet is obviously aimed at Freemasons, to induce them to leave the Craft, but it also carries a message to the children and grandchildren of Freemasons, a message I have seen nowhere else. They are told of a way to rid themselves of life's problems. The following is a direct quotation, but the italics are mine:

"Masonry is idolatry! If you *or your ancestors* have been in it, *your problems may be caused* by the generational curse (Exodus 20:15), so Jesus should be asked to lift it." (Exodus 20:15 is "Thou shalt not steal," so the author probably means Exodus 20:5: "Thou shalt not bow down thyself to them [graven images], nor serve them: for I the Lord thy God am a jealous God, visiting the iniquity of the fathers upon the children unto the third and fourth generation of them that hate me.")

In the corporate world, such a publication would lead to a fast lawsuit for libelous damage. It is deliberately malicious and uses viciously concocted lies without hesitation. Its purposes are to damage reputations, forestall membership, and encourage present members to resign. All of this is materially damaging, even without regard to the obvious impairment of fund drives for Masonic charities. Unfortunately, as mentioned earlier, Freemasonry makes a wonderful target because it has a long history of never answering critics. One can only dream of what a million-dollar judgment against these fanatics would do to curb them all.

In the meantime, by 1992 a fundamentalist faction had managed, after years of struggle, to take control of the largest Protestant denomination in the United States. It has launched what is potentially the most damaging assault on Masonry in the past century.

9

The Southern Baptist Convention

"FRIEND AGAINST FRIEND, brother against brother . . ." is frequently quoted to characterize the conflict of the American Civil War, the War Between the States. It could just as well be used to describe the current situation among the Southern Baptists.

As this is being written, toward the end of 1992, no conflict has brought more turmoil, anger, and confusion to more Masons than events surrounding the Southern Baptist Convention in Indianapolis, Indiana, in June 1992. That convention considered allegations that Freemasonry is not compatible with Christianity. The convention ordered an investigation of those charges, the results to be brought before the convention for action in Houston, Texas, in June 1993.

Current events are usually avoided by authors and publishers as "dated" material. There is no question that by the time some people read this book, the 1993 convention will have taken place, a vote taken on the allegations against Masonry, and an official position announced. That decision may demand that the Southern Baptist Masons choose between their church and their Masonic affiliation.

Upon reflection, I realized this was the most serious threat to Freemasonry in this century. It will live as part of Masonic history, regardless of the outcome, and should be set down. As one pursuing Masonic research, I have often wished that some chronicler had written down events as they were happening. It is history unfolding, and worth recording for those who come after.

What makes the problem so serious is the number of Masons involved. Polls taken by Southern Baptist bodies have found that within the thirty-eight thousand Southern Baptist churches, 14 percent of the pastors, 13 percent of the directors of missions, and 18 percent of the church deacon chairmen are, or have been, Freemasons. If Masons are correct that approximately half a million Masons are Southern Baptists, that would involve about 20 percent of all the Freemasons in the United States. The five thousand ministers who are Masons would be most seriously affected, since their professional ministry provides the means by which they support their families.

From a financial standpoint, both sides of this controversy stand to lose. If the Masons resign from Masonry, the fraternity will lose up to 20 percent of its income base, as well as millions of dollars the Baptist Masons contribute to Masonic charities.

On the other hand, if those half million Masons (and their families) leave the Southern Baptist churches for Baptist churches with a more moderate attitude, the Southern Baptists will take serious losses. Using a figure of $10 per week (which I am assured is quite low) as the church contribution of the average Baptist Mason family, the loss to the Southern Baptist churches would be in excess of $250 million per year. That could very well happen, because many Baptist Masons have told me that if the convention in 1993 takes the recommended actions against Masonry, that will be ample proof for them that the current Southern Baptist Convention does not represent the churches and the doctrines they grew up with and in which they found salvation. Does that mean that the Southern Baptist Convention has changed recently? Yes, it most definitely has, and that claim requires some supporting background.

For a dozen years a hard-core fundamentalist faction struggled to gain control of the Southern Baptist Convention, and a couple of years ago it finally succeeded. As an example of the swift exercise of power, the new leaders fired the entire Southern Baptist press and public relations staff, replacing them with people who met the new rigid standards of political and religious correctness imposed by the leadership. The new dogmatic attitude led to substantial changes, which did not go unnoticed by the popular public television host Bill Moyers, who devoted an entire sixty-minute program to observing distressing changes in the faith in which he himself is an ordained minister.

One major change is a movement away from independence of individual conscience, which previously had given the individual Southern Baptist a wide latitude in interpreting the scriptures, in doctrine that declared ". . . every man a priest." What in the past was called leadership is now being characterized as control. This is not my own imagination at work. The September 2, 1992, edition of the *Tennessee Baptist and Reflector* reported on a meeting of "conservative" (fundamentalist) leaders held in Memphis, Tennessee, on August 20, 1992. The story began: "MEMPHIS—Baptist leaders from about 15 states met here August 20 to learn how to extend 'conservative' control to the state convention level."

In other words, having achieved control of the national Southern Baptist Convention, they were now seeking control of each of the state conventions. How? The article stated, "Among the how-to strategies shared by the state leaders were: electing sympathetic state convention officers, influencing denominational appointments on the national and state levels, picking and instructing messengers (delegates) from local churches, and influencing Baptist business on the association level."

No fundamentalist power-seekers have ever been known to say, "We have enough power, so we're going to stop now." That worries many non-Mason Southern Baptists, who know that control of individual churches cannot be far behind.

Mindful, perhaps, of Lord Acton's observation that "All power corrupts, and absolute power corrupts absolutely," many moderate Baptists have left the Southern Baptists for less dictatorial Baptist churches. More have elected to stay put and fight. What they will be fighting for is to preserve the traditional autonomy of the individual church, a doctrine which had made the Southern Baptists perhaps the most democratic of all the Protestant denominations. Historically,

Southern Baptists have embraced freedom of religion and religious tolerance, but now the Freemasons have been attacked and condemned for espousing precisely those beliefs.

The purpose of the annual Southern Baptist Convention is to bring together "messengers," or delegates, from those autonomous churches to discuss matters of common interest. In theory, each church is represented. In practice, fewer than half of them have messengers present at the convention. Small churches simply cannot afford to pay the plane fare, hotel bills, and other expenses incurred during the three-day convention. Recent changes permit the largest churches to qualify to send more than one messenger. Unfortunately, what was intended to be totally democratic has turned into a convention controlled by the larger, wealthier congregations.

In theory, the actions of the convention are intended to be "executive, not legislative." The convention is never to interfere in the autonomous government of the individual church. That, however, appears to be precisely the goal of a leading faction in the faith. It began on relatively save ground, by barring churches from accepting homosexuals. It was safe because almost all Southern Baptists are opposed to homosexual behavior. The action taken was prompted by the decisions of two North Carolina churches. One church decided to bless the union of two homosexual members; the other endorsed a homosexual seminarian for the ministry.

The prohibition against homosexuals will be voted upon as a constitutional change in the 1993 Southern Baptist Convention assembly. The *Indianapolis Star* reported that "the move to change the SBC constitution was historic . . ." as indeed it was, since that constitution has not been changed for over a hundred years. The resolution was so popular that most missed the point that a restriction had been placed on church autonomy.

Changes were also made in the administration of the Foreign Missions Board. During the convention, the Reverend Keith R. Parks, director of the Southern Baptist Foreign Missions Board for twelve years, announced that he was leaving the post. In the face of what he and others felt was an extraordinary need for missionary work in Eastern Europe, fundamentalist trustees of the board had moved to cut off financial support for some of their own missionaries and foreign church leaders who did not rigidly conform to fundamentalist theology. Along with the Reverend Mr. Parks, the Foreign Missions Board vice presidents for Europe, Africa, and the Middle East also resigned. In explaining the reasons for his resignation, Rev. Keith Parks told the press that a past "atmosphere of trust and respect for differences of viewpoints has been replaced by suspicion, distrust, criticism and intimidation."

It was in that atmosphere that a number of anti-Masonic fundamentalist Baptists decided that the time was probably right for a Southern Baptist condemnation of Freemasonry.

In 1991, a sworn enemy of Freemasonry introduced a resolution to the Southern Baptist Convention asking that Freemasonry be condemned as anti-Christian. He was Dr. James L. Holly, a physician from Beaumont, Texas, and president of Mission and Ministry to Men, Inc., which he had apparently founded. As with that same resolution which he had previously brought before the convention in 1985, Dr. Holly's proposal was referred to the Interfaith Witness Department of the Home Missions Board in Atlanta. That department was created to examine other religious beliefs and doctrines, to compare them to the Christian teachings of the Southern Baptists.

On each occasion, the Home Missions Board declined to make such an investigation into Freemasonry, properly stating that Masonry is a fraternal society, not a religion, making an investigation by them inappropriate. The head of the Interfaith Witness Department commented that it was his department's function to examine religions, not fraternities. No Freemason in the Southern Baptist Church could disagree with that conclusion, and the matter appeared to have been laid to rest. And it probably would have been, had it not been for the fanatical dedication of Dr. Holly and his associates.

When control of the Southern Baptist Convention was taken over by the fundamentalist faction, an atmosphere had been created which was much more likely to entertain Dr. Holly's resolution. And Holly did try again in 1992, but this time with extensive preparation.

He wrote a sixty-page anti-Masonic booklet, which he called *Southern Baptist Convention and Masonry*. It was published by his Mission and Ministry to Men, Inc., and sent to about five thousand Baptist leaders who were expected to attend the June 1992 convention in Indianapolis. The drum-beating began with the announcement that the question of Freemasonry's compatibility with Christianity would be included on the convention's agenda. Three weeks before the convention, Dr. Holly was quoted by the Associated Press as saying that Masonry was a pagan belief that rivaled Christianity. He told one reporter, "Ninety-nine percent of Masons have no concept about what they're involved in . . . They see it as a good ole boy way of doing charitable works and getting away from the wife for a while, but they don't see how anti-Christian it is."

Before the convention, letters to the editor appeared in state publications (the Southern Baptists have no national publication). One letter in defense of Masonry, pointing out the errors in Dr. Holly's book, was written by Fred W. McPeake and sent to the Tennessee Baptist paper. Mr. McPeake is a 33rd degree Mason who had been elected a messenger to the 1992 convention. In response, he received a letter directly from a Baptist minister in his state. It is worth quoting (with no changes):

". . . I am apposed to Freemasonary . . . I have done an in-depth study of Masonary along with other pagan religions." (We can only regret that the writer did not probe Masonry deeply enough to learn how to spell it, but this mastery of the language is not an issue here.) He continues, "Masonary is a religion and opposed to Christianity. It violates the scriptures in several points. It uses fear and deception to control its members. It is also racially bigoted. It makes its members to swear oaths that are contrary to the Bible (James 5:12). It produced Joseph Smith the founder of Mormonism, which uses many of the same 'secret' signs and symbols of the Masons."

There's more in the same vein, but I will finish with the final point of the letter: "Please do yourself a favor, renounce Masonary, (baalism), or get out of the Church."

When Fred McPeake arrived at the convention, he learned that in addition to the five thousand anti-Masonic books sent by mail to Baptist leaders, Dr. Holly's followers had distributed five thousand more at the convention hall. He had a new experience when a stranger walked up to him, pointing at the little Shrine emblem on his lapel. "Take off that symbol of Satan," was the exhortation, "or leave this convention."

Outside the convention center, a member of the Church of God was picketing with a sign that read, "Baptist preachers are Anti-Christ." Early in the session a Southern Baptist from Texas bought a full-page advertisement in the *Indianapolis News* that accused the about-to-be-elected president of the convention of serious sinning, because he had saddled his church with mortgage debt incurred in construction of a new, larger building. Christian brotherly love was taking something of a beating.

Brotherhood certainly was not restored as Dr. James L. Holly rose to introduce his much-trumpeted resolution against Freemasonry. So that there will not be any misquotes or misunderstandings, here is the complete text of Dr. Holly's motion:

> That the Southern Baptist convention in annual session June 9–11, 1992 at Indianapolis, Indiana, directs the president elected at this convention to appoint an *ad hoc* committee for the study of the compatibility with Christianity and Southern Baptist doctrine of the organization known variously as the Masonic Lodge, Masonry, Freemasonry and/or Ancient and Accepted Rite of Freemasonry. The study is to encompass any and all branches and/or lodges thereof. Furthermore, the Convention directs the president to appoint this committee within thirty days of the conclusion of this Convention and to charge this committee with the responsibility of bringing a report with recommendation to the convention which is to meet in Houston, Texas [in] June 1993.

Dr. Holly, of course, volunteered to serve on the ad hoc investigating committee, as did the well-known TV evangelist Rev. John Ankerberg, the messenger from the Brainerd Baptist church in Chattanooga, Tennessee. For many years John Ankerberg has been a professional anti-Mason ("professional" in the sense that he produces and peddles tracts, books, audiotapes, and even a videotape about the Master Mason degree, all of which combine to produce a steady flow of income for his strange ministry). Dr. Holly demanded that no

Freemason Baptist be allowed on the committee, which was rather like asking that the entire jury be selected from among the friends and relative of the prosecuting attorney.

The president of the SBC allowed just fifteen minutes for discussion of Dr. Holly's motion. The only person called on to speak in favor of Masonry was Fred McPeake, who was given all of two minutes to address eighteen thousand messengers about an issue affecting up to half a million Freemason Baptists. The rest of the quarter hour was given to Dr. Holly and a colleague of his from his home state of Texas.

One man left standing silent before the microphone was Marion Reed, a 33rd degree Mason and editor of Kentucky's *Masonic Home Journal*. Other messengers from his state included three Past Grand Masters of Kentucky Masons, but none of them had a chance to speak.

An ad hoc committee made up of anti-Masons would, of course, have been the kiss of death for any hope of a scholarly and fair investigation, but on that point Dr. Holly was disappointed. Before his motion could be put to a vote, an amendment to the motion was introduced by messenger Alvin Rowe of Florida and was approved. It read:

> That the Southern Baptist Convention in annual session June 9–11 at Indianapolis, Indiana, directs the Interfaith Witness Department of the Home Missions Board to study the compatibility with Christianity and Southern Baptist Doctrine of the organization known variously as the Masonic Lodge, Masonry, Freemasonry, and/or Ancient and Accepted Rite of Freemasonry. The study is to encompass any and all branches and/or lodges thereof. Furthermore, the Convention charges the Home Missions Board with the responsibility of bringing a report with recommendation to the Convention which is to meet in Houston, Texas, June 15–17, 1993.

So the Interfaith Witness Department, which had twice taken the stand that Freemasonry is a fraternity, not a religion, was ordered to conduct the investigation which it had rejected in 1985 and 1991. After the vote, a spokesman repeated the board's stand on the inappropriateness of such an investigation by the Home Missions Board, but he was curtly silenced by the president, who pronounced, "The convention has spoken!"

Dr. Holly has spoken, too, making it clear that if the findings of the Interfaith Witness Department are not in keeping with his accusations against Masonry, he will have a motion ready at the 1993 convention. He will ask that the report be sent aside and that Freemasonry be condemned by a vote of the convention.

There have been indications that Holly is concerned that the study will produce findings favorable to Masonry, and his misgivings are not unfounded. There was always a chance that the investigators, in their desire to be scholarly and fair, might be swayed by the history of Southern Baptist leaders who were Freemasons, from Rev. Lansing Burrows, a Mason who was a Civil War hero and secretary of the SBC, up to men like Abner McCall, a Mason who served as president of Baylor University, the pride of Southern Baptist educators. In September 1992 Holly demanded that the Home Missions Board remove Dr. Gary Leazer, head of the Interfaith Witness Department, who was in charge of the investigation. The Home Missions Board rejected that demand.

Undeterred, Dr. Holly then appeared before members of that board with over six hundred pages of additional anti-Masonic material. He also expressed his resentment at being called an "anti-Mason." He protested that he is the Masons' best friend. He loves them, which is why he is trying so hard to save their souls, while at the same time achieving the purification of his church. *Purification.* That is precisely the word used by the papal council as the motivation for creating the Inquisition.

Nor does the comparison stop there. Reading of Dr. Holly's soul-saving ambitions, it is easy to compare his attitude with that of a Dominican torturer, who bends over his burned, broken, and bloody victim on the rack to say (with a gentle smile), "My son, your soul is much more important than your body. We're doing this to you because we love you!" Sure.

To get a better grasp of this whole situation, it is necessary to take a good hard look at the book that Dr. Holly wrote for the express purpose of triggering this turmoil.

10

The Physician-Fanatic

I
T IS NOT disparaging to identify Dr. James L. Holly as a fanatic, since that is how he proudly labels himself.

He proclaims, as all Christian fundamentalists do, that he believes in the inerrancy of Holy Scripture. I will not argue that point, but I must take issue with his equally fervent belief in the inerrancy of his own interpretation of those Scriptures. As we shall see, Dr. Holly can wander far from the truth with his tedious speculations as to what the Scriptures *really* means.

To one looking from the outside, his most distinguishing trait is his total confidence in his own intelligence and knowledge, which he believes are infinitely superior to those of the thousands of Southern Baptist ministers who have sought the fraternal bonds of Masonic membership. There is no question in his mind that he is a lot smarter than they are. He, not they, *knows* what God wants, and he so frequently presents specific directives from the Almighty that one might imagine that the two of them have regular weekly meetings.

Far more remarkable is the fact that the fundamentalist faction in the Southern Baptist leadership apparently accepts what Dr. Holly says as gospel, while giving little credence to the voices of their own ministers who have been through the Masonic degrees that Holly denigrates and who know that he is not reporting the truth.

Let's deal with some specific examples from Dr. Holly's sixty-page condemnation of Freemasonry:

In the preface to his book, Dr. Holly uses—or rather misuses—Scripture to identify the Masonic threat to the Christian faith. He quotes from James 4:1: "From whence come wars and fightings among you? come they not hence, even of your lusts that war in your members?" He gives this translation of a Greek word for "war" as "a word that means 'soldiering,' the passions that disquiet the soul which are like a military encampment which is formed to make a military expedition."

Then, based solely on his unique interpretation of one word, he gives a very creative and completely erroneous interpretation of that entire verse. "James 4:1," he writes, "really states that Christians have allowed a military force to bivouac in their lives and homes. But, unlike the temporary bivouac, this encampment has become a permanent installation. The 'camp' has become a fort." That's where Masonry comes in:

"The church has also allowed 'an alien military force' into her membership. This 'military force'—the membership of the Masonic Lodge—is pledged to another general and works for the glory and honor of a foreign god. Until they are dislodged from the church, the Lodge will continue to disrupt God's plan and desire to revive his people."

With this corruption of Holy Scripture Holly has implanted a fear, and he suggests the solution that will rid his church of the enemy. It is from this "scriptural" base that he bestows on himself the duty and authority to condemn Freemasonry as anti-Christian.

Before we move on to those more detailed condemnations, let us take a look at his scriptural authority:

James 4:1 has absolutely nothing to do with a foreign military encampment. The world "member" as used in the King James Version means "body parts," as in James 3:5, which says, "Even so the tongue is a little member. . . ." James 4:1 refers to *lusts of the body*, sensual lust. Dr. Holly takes "members" to mean members of a congregation, or "membership." That is a complete (and probably deliberate) distortion. Nor am I pitting my personal interpretation against his. For bible study I use *Cruden's Complete Concordance.* At the beginning of the section headed "member" it says, *"Generally used in the archaic sense of limb, or other part of the body."*

Had Dr. Holly taken us a little further into this same scriptural letter, he might have cited James 4:4, which begins, "Ye adulterers and adulteresses . . ."

I am not going to call attention here to every malicious twist of the true meaning of the Scripture that Holly uses in his attempts to denounce Masonry; but the general issue is so important that it is worth reinforcing this statement as to his distortion of the Epistle of James 4:1.

The updated translation of James 4:1 in the New English Bible (and the Oxford Study Bible) is, "What causes conflicts and quarrels among you? Do they not spring from the aggressiveness of your bodily desires?" Not a single enemy military encampment in sight.

It is interesting, by the way, to read the biblical scholars' update of James 3:1. It might have been written for Dr. James Holly: "My brothers, not many of you should become teachers, for you may be certain that we who teach shall ourselves be judged with greater strictness." I agree. I have spent all my life with the King James version, and I have no intention of switching to the Doctor James version.

Take his description of the third degree, the degree that makes a man a Master Mason. In the drama of his ceremony, Hiram, the master builder of Solomon's temple, is struck down by three assassins who bury him in a nondescript grave in the wilderness. When the grave is discovered, King Solomon orders that Hiram's body be dug up and moved to a more respectable grave at Jerusalem. In this degree, technically the highest in all of Freemasonry, *there is no mention of resurrection,* simply the re-burying of a dead body. This is not a religious ceremony in any way and, like the other Masonic degrees, offers *no means of salvation.* These facts are easily proven by referring to any of the numerous exposés of Masonic ritual available at any well-stocked public library.

But not according to Dr. Holly. He says, "Masons go through a death and resurrection ritual in the Master Mason degree. Membership is dated from the time they were 'raised,' resurrected or saved, by membership in the Lodge. Salvation is maintained through faithful membership in the lodge."

Thousands of Southern Baptist ministers are Freemasons, and they have all been through the third degree. Ask them their opinion of Dr. Holly's version of the Master Mason's degree, and every one of them will say that his description is one big blatant lie.

To set the stage for his ongoing diatribe on the evils of Masonry, Dr. Holly asserts that he will quote Masonic authorities. "Albert Pike, Albert G. Mackey and W. L. Wilmshurst," he asserts, "are embraced by Masons as authorities on Freemasonry. They can speak of the real intent of the secret society of Freemasonry." No, they can't. Let's look at each of those authors individually.

Much has already been said in this book about Albert Pike, of whom Dr. Holly also says, "The acceptance of Albert Pike [who has been dead for over a hundred years] . . . as an authority on Freemasonry is universally affirmed."

I have already quoted the Scottish Rite Supreme Council's preface to Pike's *Morals and Dogma*, which states that "Everyone is entirely free to reject and dissent from whatsoever herein may seem to him to be untrue or unsound." Confirming Pike's limited audience, the preface also clearly establishes that *Morals and Dogma* was written "for the Southern Jurisdiction [of the Scottish Rite] of the United States." A targeted readership of fewer than 10 percent of Freemasons is a far cry from being "universally affirmed." Dr. Holly would have been on firmer ground had he said, "Pike *used to be* an authority to *some* Masons over a century ago."

Albert G. Mackey was born in 1807, qualified as a doctor of medicine, and began his writing career in 1834. He, too, does not merit Dr. Holly's label as one of those who are "embraced by Masons as an authority of Freemasonry." Two modern Masonic authorities are historians Fred L. Pick and G. Norman Knight. In writing about Albert G. Mackey in their reference book for Freemasons, they write, ". . . his writings, taken as 'gospel' in his lifetime, have come to be recognized as unreliable in very many respects."

Walter L. Wilmshurst, an English Mason, was born in 1867. His book, *The Meaning of Masonry*, is—like many Masonic books—

largely an expression of his own personal opinions. By no means is Wilmshurst "embraced by Masons" as an authority. In the course of writing this book, I asked about twenty American Masons, many of whom I consider to be knowledgeable, their opinion of the writings of W. L. Wilmshurst. Without exception, they responded that they had never heard of him.

One must wonder why Dr. Holly dwells so much on Masonic writers of generations ago and does not seek information from current Masonic writers who *are* universally recognized as authorities: the prolific Masonic author, Allen Roberts; the Masonic scholar, Professor Wallace McLeod; or the librarian of the United Grand Lodge of England, John Hamill, for example.

Why doesn't Dr. Holly contact such men, or quote their writings? Because they won't provide what he wants to hear. It is easier for him to go back a century and more, perhaps taking the view that "authorities" then must be authorities now. If that were true, I could trace the faith of the Southern Baptist Convention back to early "authorities" and present profuse quotations of Holy Scripture to prove conclusively that Jesus Christ wholeheartedly approved of the institution of slavery. Wasn't the reason for the founding of the Southern Baptist Convention in 1845 that Baptists in the South disagreed with the antislavery attitudes and actions of Baptists in the North?

Do Southern Baptists *today* believe that Jesus Christ favors slavery? Of course not. The point is that if one is determined to condemn a group of men of today, credibility requires that one quote the authorities of today.

As a well-qualified anti-Mason, James Holly happily cites the forged document by Léo Taxil, in which Albert Pike purportedly affirmed that "Lucifer is God." This is almost a requirement for any Mason-hater, as is disclaiming any knowledge that Taxil openly confessed to forging the document.

Dr. Holly also follows the accepted line of condemning Masonry for having *secrets*, then triumphantly reveals to the reader just what those secrets are. His cohort, the Reverend John Ankerberg, the Southern Baptist fundamentalist evangelist, employs the same technique. Ankerberg published a book called *The Secrets of the Masonic Lodge*. When are these men, and others like them, going to admit that if they can know all the Masonic "secrets" and publish them for all to see, then there obviously *aren't* any Masonic secrets?

Holly actually goes further than others. He shares his wisdom that "there is nothing done in secret which is honorable and noble. All that is done in secret is selfish, sinful or Satanic." Does that mean that I should stop drinking Coca-Cola because its secret formula makes it satanic?

Perhaps the most important "secret" of Masonry that Dr. Holly wants to share with his readers is one degree of the Southern Jurisdiction of Scottish Rite. He writes, "This presentation focuses upon the thirtieth degree of Scottish Rite because it is clearly the most occultic."

Before we discuss Dr. Holly's creative twistings of the true meanings of that degree, we should take an unbiased look at what the degree really is, to form a basis for comparison. A bit of historical background will be necessary for a full understanding.

The Knights Templar were members of a religious order of military monks formed in 1118, in the aftermath of the First Crusade. All men of the knightly class, the Templars took lifetime vows of poverty, chastity, and obedience. Upon entering the order, they gave all their worldly goods, including lands and buildings, to the order. Their purpose was to devote their entire lives to fighting for the True Cross in the Holy Land. During their two hundred years of existence, over twenty thousand Knights Templar died on the holy battlefield, fighting the Muslim enemy. When not in armor, the Templar wore the simple white robe of a monk, with a red cross sewn over the left breast.

A good example of the Templars' devotion to Christ occurred at the loss of their castle at Safed to the Egyptian sultan Baibars. Breaking his promise of freedom in exchange for surrender, the sultan gave the two-hundred-man Templar garrison a choice. Each knight could choose to convert to Islam and live, or cling to his Christian faith and have his head struck off. Every one of the Templar knights chose to kneel before his Muslim executioner and lose his head, rather than lose his faith in Jesus Christ.

The downfall of the order came about from its wealth. Through-out its existence it had accumulated great assets. There were all the "dowries" willingly handed over by the thousands of men who took their Templar vows, as well as generous gifts from kings and nobles to support their endeavors. And in addition the Templar share of the loot taken after each successful battle all went into the Templar treasury.

One who lusted after that treasure was King Philip IV of France, who was constantly short of funds because of his incessant wars with Edward I of England. Philip had borrowed huge sums from the Templar order, and he resented being indebted to monks who exercised so much influence. He wanted the Templar treasury, and he wanted those debts wiped out.

Philip's chance presented itself after he had managed to maneuver his own man onto the Throne of Peter as Pope Clement V, who moved the seat of the Church from Rome to France, where it remained for the next seventy-five years. The king's carefully organized plan to have every Templar in France arrested on the same day gave rise to a new superstition that lives today. The ill-fated Templars in France were arrested on Friday the thirteenth, in October of 1307. They were immediately turned over to the Inquisition, and their torture for confessions of heresy began on that same day. All of the hideous skills of the medieval torturer were turned loose on the Christian Templars. Hot irons were applied to all parts of their bodies. Teeth were wrenched out and sockets probed to increase the pain. Many had their feet burned off over pans of glowing charcoal.

In those days, a confession extracted under torture was valid in the eyes of the Church. Any attempt by a prisoner to retract his confession after the torture stopped was sufficient to brand him a "relapsed heretic." The punishment for that crime was to be burned at the stake. Many Templars were.

The most memorable Templar to meet that agonizing end was the aging Grand Master of the order, Jacques de Molay. Watching stronger, younger knights caving in to the torture, and in many cases dying from its excesses, the grand master became convinced that he would not be able to survive such treatment. To save himself from the inquisitors, de Molay confessed to several counts of heresy. Instead of leading his order and setting an example, he had betrayed it, thus violating his own vows.

In 1312, five years after the torture began, Pope Clement V dissolved the order of Knights Templar by papal decree, admitting that the inquisitors had not provided sufficient "proof" of heresy within the ranks of the military monks to find them guilty of that charge. He ordered that all of their property be given to their rivals, the military order of the Hospitallers of St. John of Jerusalem (The Knights of Malta). Jacques de Molay, with several other Templar officers, was held in prison for another two years, then sentenced to life imprisonment.

Both church and state were disturbed by rumors spreading throughout France, rumors claiming that the suppression of the Templars was not in accordance with God's will, but was simply a bloody example of a joint royal and papal plot for self-enrichment. To put those rumors to rest, a high platform was erected in front of Notre Dame Cathedral in Paris. Jacques de Molay was ordered to mount the platform to make public the sins of which his order was guilty. The whole world was invited to hear the old man confess that the Knights Templar had rejected Christianity.

De Molay knew that if he retracted his false confession, he was condemning himself to be burned alive at the stake, but from some hidden source he summoned the courage to obey his conscience and speak the truth. His speech is part of Masonic education:

> I think it only right that at so solemn a moment, when my life has so little time to run, I should reveal the deception which has been practiced and speak up for the truth. Before heaven and earth and all of you here as my witnesses, I admit that I am guilty of the grossest iniquity. But the iniquity is that I lied in admitting the disgusting charges laid against the Order. I declare, and I must declare, that the Order is innocent. Its purity and saintliness are beyond question. I have indeed confessed that the Order is guilty, but I have done so only to save myself from terrible tortures by saying what my enemies wished me to say. Other knights who have retracted their confessions have been led to the stake, yet the thought of

> dying is not so awful that I shall confess to four crimes
> which have never been committed. Life is offered to
> me, but at the price of infamy. At such a price, life is
> not worth having. I do not grieve that I must die if life
> can be brought only by piling one lie upon another.

After this shocking outburst, Jacques de Molay was hustled off the platform and taken to a little island in the River Seine for his execution. Legend has it that as the flames were roasting the flesh from his bones, he cried out a curse on King Philip and Pope Clement V, calling for each of them to meet him for judgment before the throne of God before the year was out. Within the year, both were dead.

In the Southern Jurisdiction 30th degree, the ceremony that recounts this historical drama, the candidate is led into a tomb with three skulls on display. The skull on the left wears a crown; the one in the center bears a laurel wreath; and the third wears a papal tiara. The skull bearing the wreath of the hero is Jacques de Molay. The skull with the crown represents Philip IV, a secular tyrant, while the third represents Clement V, a religious tyrant. The candidate is told that he should always oppose tyranny in whatever form, whether it emanates from a government or from a religion. He is told that this will be "for the good of humanity."

In spite of this very clear-cut message, Dr. Holly doesn't hesitate to present his own contrived interpretation of the Masonic drama of the thirtieth degree. The setting, he writes, does not have "the ornaments of a Christian service." Of course not: It is not a religious service, Christian or otherwise. It is an attempt to portray in dramatic form a landmark event in history, and to learn from it. The lesson learned is that rampant tyranny is a danger to all mankind. And since that event represented a joint persecution by monarchy and papacy, it speaks to the wisdom of separating church and state, then opposing tyranny from either source.

I can see nothing in the lessons of this degree that Southern Baptists could object to, since they repeatedly have affirmed their belief in the separation of church and state. Every history of the Baptist Church that I have seen devotes substantial space to the persecution of Baptists by church-partnered governments, and even by the Inquisition. It is easy to imagine a devout Baptist nodding his head in total agreement with the lessons extracted from a brutal history of Christian torture and death.

Dr. Holly, on the other hand, feels he is smart enough to detect different truths behind the dramatic symbols. He sees the skull and tiara representing Pope Clement V as "the vicarious representation of the Church of Jesus Christ. . . ." Instead of condemning religious tyranny, as the candidates for the 30th degree are admonished to do, Holly asserts, on no grounds whatsoever, that they are really devoted to condemning the Church of Jesus Christ. He claims that the deepest secrets of Freemasonry are not revealed until the man "vows upon his death loyalty to the Lodge above all else, including the church and Jesus Christ." That goes beyond perverting the truth; it is simply an outrageous lie. Every Mason is told repeatedly throughout his Masonic career that, no matter how high the level he achieves within the fraternity, he is *never* to put his duties and responsibilities to the lodge higher than his responsibilities and obligations to his own church. I know of no instance in which that admonition has been violated.

Since Dr. Holly's book states that it focuses on the 30th degree of Scottish Rite, we should probably discuss the other parts of that degree. Having established a position against tyranny and in favor of the separation of church and state, the degree suggests that *one* contributor to tyranny is ignorance (the lack of education) for all too often ignorance makes men easier to deceive and control. To dramatize this point, the candidate is encouraged to continue with his own search for knowledge (*secular* knowledge) by being shown a decorative ladder with the steps named for the ancient and classical components of the liberal arts. These are Grammar, Rhetoric, Logic, Arithmetic, Geometry, Astronomy, and Music (*not* Theology). This presentation of past quests for knowledge is simply symbolic of the need for every Mason constantly to expand his own knowledge and to help others to do the same. That charge is the inspiration for thousands of scholarships which have been funded by Masons across the country, and which are awarded on the basis of need and merit, without regard to race, national origin, or religious creed.

In the chambers prepared for the drama of the 30th degree there is a knight in a coffin. He represents all the knights who were killed in this historical act of persecution, although there are those who feel that he symbolizes *all* of the Christians who died at the hands of their persecutors. (If so, he also represents a great number of victims who were Baptists.)

Dr. Holly asks, "Who does that knight in the coffin represent? Albert Pike says that the answer lies in the mysteries of the Kaballa." No, he doesn't, but Holly presents this conclusion without citation or explanation. Instead, he immediately and deliberately misquotes Albert Mackey, from *Mackey's Revised Encyclopedia of Freemasonry*.

Mackey was citing the origins of the ancient Judaic system of Kabbalah as represented by scholars, especially Dr. Christian David Ginsburg, who had written a book on the subject in 1863. Mackey *quotes Dr. Ginsburg*, introducing that quote with these words, which Holly chose to omit:

"In what estimation the Kabbala is held by Jewish scholars, we may learn from the tradition which they teach, and which Dr. Ginsburg has given in his exhaustive work (Kaballah, 84) in the following words . . ." (Now follows the quote used by Holly, who presents it erroneously as the writings of a Freemason, instead of citing it as a passage from the work of a non-Masonic scholar, which in fact it is.):

"The Kaballah was first taught by God to a select company of angels, who formed a theosophic school in Paradise. After the fall, the angels most graciously communicated this heavenly doctrine to the disobedient children of the earth."

If Dr. Holly had delved a bit deeper into Kabbalistic lore, he would know that these angels who taught the "disobedient children of the earth" were not among the angels who fell, but were among those who stayed loyal to God in Heaven. They taught after *the* fall, not *their* fall. Perhaps Holly did know it and just didn't want to mess up his tedious thesis, which requires that these angels be numbered with the fallen.

"The only angels to be cast out of heaven," he declares, "were those who joined Lucifer in his rebellion against God. This select group of angels had to be those who rebelled with Lucifer and were cast out of heaven." (*Had to be?* Only to fit the hateful compulsions of James L. Holly.)

Dr. Holly goes on to quote five more paragraphs from Dr. Ginsburg's discourse on what traditional Jewish Kabbalists (*not* Freemasons) believed. He correctly quotes Dr. Ginsburg's history of the development of the Kabbalah with "No one, however, dared to write it down until Simon ben Jochai." Simon ben Jochai was a rabbi who lived at the time of the destruction of the second Temple in A.D. 70. Upon being condemned to death by the Roman emperor Titus, he sought refuge, along with his sons and disciples, by hiding in a cavern.

When the rabbi died, Kabbalists believe that a "dazzling light" filled the cavern, with a burning fire outside, guarding the entrance. "As they were preparing for his obsequies, a voice was heard from heaven. . . ." Note that the voice was *from* heaven."

"Who was this man?" wonders Holly. To find the answer, he writes, "The truth? Mackey states . . ." (and, once again, he goes on to quote Ginsburg, not Mackey):

"And when the remains were deposited in the tomb, another voice was heard from heaven, saying, 'This is he who caused the earth to quake and the kingdoms to shake.' " To the Kabbalist, these words *from heaven* are identifying the speaker, *not* Rabbi Simon ben Jochai. The voice is the voice of God, referring to Himself as "he who caused the earth to quake and the kingdoms to shake." Simon ben Jochai is presented as a man who has found favor with God.

Now, we finally get to the point: the conclusions that Dr. Holly draws from this twisted, irrelevant pseudo-research. He invents a totally irrational and unfounded discovery to share with his Southern Baptist readers: "Who was Simon ben Jochai? He was one and the same as in Isaiah 14:12. He was Lucifer or one of his demons disguised in the form of a man." Nothing Holly has discussed is even remotely related to the drama of the Knights Templar or the murder of Jacques de Molay, or the lessons learned in the 30th degree — except in the mind of James L. Holly. Now he reveals the rare jewel, the fantastic product of his imaginary findings: "Who does the man in the coffin in the thirtieth degree represent? He is the Simon ben Jochai of the Kabballa. He is Lucifer himself, or one of his demons."

This is a superb example of the lowest level of propagandist deception. Dr. Holly knows precisely where he wants to end up. He knows what he wants to "prove," but he can't see a clear path to get there because there are no facts to support him. The only solution is to lie, to indulge in unfounded speculation, to misquote in order to establish, at whatever the cost, that somewhere in the Scottish Rite 30th degree is Satan himself. Why not? He's not likely to get caught. Holly's followers never question that he is telling the truth, and he is even quite likely to earn praise for the depth and complexity of his research. Let's review it:

First, he has involved the Kabbalah, a theosophic system developed by Orthodox rabbinical scholars, beginning in the seventh century. Then he misquotes Albert Pike to contrive a connection. Next, Holly pretends that he is quoting the beliefs and teachings of Masonic encyclopaedist Albert Mackey, although every quotation cited was actually written by Dr. Ginsburg, who in turn was not stating his own beliefs, but rather was explaining the beliefs of ancient traditional Kabbalists. Those beliefs are extended to the legendary life and death of Simon ben Jochai, a first-century rabbi.

In the Kabbalistic tradition, a voice "*from* heaven" speaks at the tomb bearing the remains of Rabbi Simon ben Jochai. Out of this event Holly fabricates the notion, totally unsupported by written evidence or reference, that Rabbi Simon ben Jochai *must* be "Lucifer or one of his demons." Reason is sent reeling.

But after bludgeoning the facts so as to make Satan replace the rabbi, what proof does Holly offer to link any of that with the 30th degree in Scottish Rite Masonry? Clearly none at all; but he has come this far and is now desperate to show that Rabbi Simon ben Jochai was Lucifer, or Lucifer himself, or one of Lucifer's demons, is in that coffin! Lacking the tiniest shred of evidence to back such a theory, no historian or scholar, or any honest man, could find his way out of the dilemma, but there is always a way out for the fanatic: Just *say* it. Forget about logic, proof, reason, circumstantial evidence, or even a vague suggestion of a connection. Just go ahead and say it confidently enough times to establish the erroneous fact that Satan is in a Masonic degree. Ignore the facts and trumpet the triumphant lie that Freemasons worship Satan!

At another point in the 30th degree the candidate recites an oath that includes the vow ". . . to strive unceasingly for the happiness of fellow beings, for the propagation of light [knowledge] and for the overthrow of superstition, fanaticism, imposture and intolerance." Dr. Holly declares that this oath is ". . . in reality an oath to work for the destruction of Christianity." In the 30th degree this lesson warns Masons of the evils of *superstition, fanaticism, imposture*, and *intolerance*. Dr. Holly declares that "each of these is a synonym of revealed, God-centered religion."

The Mason understands *superstition* to be an irrational belief, like not stepping on cracks in the sidewalk, or walking under a ladder, or knocking on wood. Dr. Holly (alone) claims that the Masons use the word *superstition* to mean the true word of God. He argues that *religious tolerance* is offensive to God, who demands intolerance of all Christians. He states that Jesus wants every Christian to be a fanatic, thus rendering *fanaticism* a Christian virtue. He doesn't attempt to explain how *imposture*, a word meaning "fraud" or "deceit," could possibly be linked synonymously with any revealed God-centered religion (unless, perhaps, knowing that he himself is guilty of gross imposture, he forgives it on the basis that everything he says or does is automatically devoutly Christian).

The archbishop of Canterbury made a lecture tour in the United States during August and September of 1992. Speaking to a largely Episcopalian audience, of course, the archbishop stated: "Christianity can maintain its commitment to the uniqueness of Christ in a pluralist world, and yet still be genuinely tolerant." What a shock it will be to the Church of England to learn that the primate of the Anglican Church throughout the world is the Antichrist, for ". . . toleration is the antithesis of the Christian message." Those are the words of the bellicose Dr. Holly, who espouses a doctrine that is neither Christian nor American.

Holly also equates Freemasonry with communism, never explaining that every Communist party member must be an atheist, while no atheist may become a Freemason. He says that Freemasons have their own wording to indicate that they are in accord with Lenin's condemnation of religion as "the opiate of the people." Masons and Communists, he insists, are "opposed to revealed religion." That's a lie, of course, but at least the doctor quotes only Lenin, not the Masons, as saying that religion is the opiate of the people. (As a matter of fact, Lenin didn't say it, either. Karl Marx did.)

There is much more in his writings that can easily be exposed as vicious lies. Nevertheless, as one examines the work of James L. Holly one may experience a strange blend of anger, depression, frustration, and a genuine apprehension for the future of our sacred individual freedoms. This man has tasted power and influence, and they are dangerous, heady drugs. Prove him wrong, and he'll come back with other information. Vote him down and he'll get up and counterattack. The only forces that can defeat his kind are knowledge, logic, and a deep appreciation of the love, sympathy, charity, and brotherhood that were the central themes of Christ's teaching. Dr. Holly cannot possibly understand those things. His self-centered "Christianity" is aggressive, militaristic, divisive, and mean.

I may be questioned on the word "divisive," but it applies to James L. Holly. It means promoting dissension or discord, which is exactly what Holly appears to have done in two churches in his own hometown. Southern Baptists in Beaumont, Texas, have told me that he joined a local Southern Baptist church and immediately began antagonizing the pastor and criticizing other members of the church. He caused so much trouble that he was finally asked to leave.

He joined another Southern Baptist church and promptly began his program of bullying, threatening, and generally shaking up the congregation. That church, too, asked him to get out.

Holly then went back to the first church and reapplied for membership. They remembered him all too well and wanted no more of James L. Holly. His application was rejected.

Now it would seem that what he did to those two churches he wants to do so the entire Southern Baptist Convention.

His twisted "findings" provide ample evidence that Holly considers himself to be the smartest Southern Baptist of them all. Smarter than the hundreds of thousands of Masons who have experienced all the Masonic degrees, without seeing or hearing any threat to their Christian beliefs. Smarter than the thousands of Southern Baptist ministers who find no conflict between their faith and their Masonic brotherhood.

Holly lies, and he knows it. He quotes out of context, and he knows it. He distorts the truth to suit his own ends, and he knows it. How does this man qualify to be a religious leader?

Of course, even if he succeeds in driving the Freemasons out of the Southern Baptist churches and arranges for the "purification" of churches imbued with "satanic" influence because of Masonic cornerstone layings, Holly's job will be far from finished; that is, if he truly wants to rid the Southern Baptist Church entirely of all Masonic influence. Here are a few points he should consider:

Perhaps church members should refuse to recite the Pledge of Allegiance to the flag, since it was written by a Freemason (who was also a Baptist minister).

He may want to forbid any use of the flag whatsoever, since it came into the world when Freemason George Washington approached Betsy, wife of Freemason John Ross, to help design and to sew the first American flag.

He may want to forbid all Southern Baptists to sing *Onward Christian Soldiers*, since it was composed by a Freemason. And, perhaps, he may want to ban *God Bless America*. For it, too, was written by a Freemason.

Part Two

The Wayfarer
by Hieronymus Bosch

11

Masonic Origins

L AST YEAR I was the guest on a one-hour radio program that stretched into three hours because the calls kept coming. For two weeks before the program, the station made brief announcements that a show about Freemasonry would be airing, and apparently the word spread in the local Masonic lodges. Fully half the calls that came in that evening were from Masons.

To start things off, the show host asked me about my book, *Born in Blood*. I responded by explaining the theory of Masonic origins which I felt had been extensively developed through my research into British medieval history.

One of the first calls came from a Mason who said, "Your guest is way off base. I've been a Mason for fifteen years, and I can tell you that Masonry began in the building of the Egyptian pyramids."

Soon another Masonic caller said, "I've been a Mason a lot longer than the man who called a few minutes ago, and I can assure you that Masonry began in the building of Solomon's temple, under a master builder that we still honor today."

A third Mason called some time later, to put the matter to rest with, "I've been a Mason for half my life, and if you really want the truth I can tell you that Masonry was born in the medieval guilds of stonemasons who built the great Gothic cathedrals, the first of which was the Temple of Solomon."

Since the first Gothic cathedral had not been built until 1,500 years after the construction of Solomon's temple, the show host looked at me with a puzzled frown. I responded by drawing the edge of my hand across my throat, a suggestion to cut short that discussion. No one was learning anything about Masonry, except perhaps that there is no general agreement on the origins of the fraternity.

Of all the theories of Masonic beginnings, clearly the most popular is that it all started with "operative" guilds of working stonemasons. Later, nonworkers were accepted into those guilds, to become known as "speculative" Masons. They shared the "secrets" held by the master masons, which apparently included the secrets of how to build in the Gothic style. Later still, the speculative masons broke away in their own organizations, preserving the secrets of the master builders (which have now been lost and cannot be identified).

This theory apparently began with Freemasons who took the legend of Hiram Abiff to be history, and not allegory. Masonic writers of that time marveled that such a wonderful story had eluded the authors of the Old Testament. Initiates into the third degree were taught that the Hiram story was literal truth. With that base, the existence of Freemasonry at the time of the building of Solomon's temple made sense to them, as did the role of Hiram, described as the master builder of the temple, as the first Grand Master of Masonry.

Dr. James Anderson, in the first Grand Lodge constitution, adopted in 1723, stated that Masonry had started with King Athelstan in ninth-century York, in England. Later Masonic scholars could find no historical support for that theory and decided that Masonry had really begun in medieval guilds of stonemasons—ignoring the fact that there was no historic support for that theory, either.

Although devoid of documentary evidence, the medieval-builder theory took hold. At the time Freemasons revealed themselves in London in 1717, there was no documentary record of Masonic symbols: The square and compasses do not appear in Masonic writings until a generation later. The use of masons' tools to teach moral lessons appears to be also a later addition, if one requires written evidence for proof of existence. If that's true, then the day came when the theory that had produced the symbols was said to be proven by the symbols it had created!

That "proof" was not strong enough, however, to stem the flow of inventive ideas put forward on the subject of Masonic origins. Some asserted that the fraternity had been born in the ancient British Druid religion. Others claimed origins in the *steinmetzen* (stonemasons) of Germany, the Roman *Collegia*, and the *Compagnage*. Some even held out for the Culdees, an ancient order of monks which existed in Ireland and Scotland in the eighth century. The order did not find favor with the Church and died out during the tenth century, before the era of Gothic architecture.

Most recently, after all manner of investigations by Masonic researchers, Masonic scholars such as Allen Roberts in the United States and John Hamill in England have flatly stated that the simple truth is that no one knows how, where, when, or why Freemasonry was founded.

For me, that last question "Why?" was by far the most important. To find the answer to that question would be to discover the original purposes of Masonry and the reason for its survival for centuries as a secret society in Britain.

I must admit that I began my own research with the conviction that Freemasonry's original purposes had to be more serious than a social club attached to a guild of stonecutters. That did not seem a likely reason for starting a secret organization that was to survive and spread for hundreds of years.

I had only one fixed point, the Regius Manuscript dating from about 1390. The manuscript seems to establish that there was Freemasonry — or a predecessor — in fourteenth-century Britain. The implausibility of the theory of origins in medieval stonemasons' guilds became apparent after my research in England clearly established that there were no guilds of stonemasons in fourteenth-century Britain. The first stonemasons' guild was not documented until two hundred years later, in the sixteenth century.

To counter that point, some Masonic historians claim that there is indeed documentary evidence of a stonemasons' guild in the fourteenth century. They cite a set of regulations establishing rules for the conduct of the masons' trade, set by the municipal authorities in London in 1356. That, to them, is clear evidence that a guild of stonemasons was in existence at that time. However, all non-Masonic historians feel that those regulations are clear proof of the opposite, that there was *no* such guild. The reasoning is that if a stonemasons' guild had existed, it would have had the right by charter to set its own rules governing the craft. That such regulations were passed directly by the municipal authorities means that there was no guild organization through which the authorities could negotiate.

The arguments go back and forth and may never be settled because of the absence of documented proof. My own theory is that Masonry was born in a secret society formed for self-protection by fugitive Knights Templar, along with their employees and their associates, in England and Scotland, who had been found guilty of heresy and excommunicated by Pope Clement V. With their order destroyed by papal decree and themselves branded as excommunicated outlaws, the Templars who managed to escape were in extreme peril. If found, their fate would undoubtedly include torture and burning at the stake. They had a vital need for passwords, recognition signals, and secret meetings. (All of the circumstantial evidence I found to support that theory is presented in detail in *Born in Blood*.) Some Masons agreed with my findings, and some disagreed, so that my theory simply took its place alongside a dozen others, and new theories continue to be brought forward.

Early in 1991, I was honored by an invitation to the annual banquet of the Philalethes Society, a Masonic research and education organization. The principal speaker was Cyril Batham, long a member of the prestigious Quatuor Coronati Lodge of Research in England, the premier Masonic research lodge of the world. Mr. Batham surprised us all by explaining his own theory of Masonic origins, a totally original concept.

Mr. Batham believes that Masonry began in a secret society formed by dispossessed monks after the dissolution of the monasteries in England. As a major part of his break with the church hierarchy in Rome, Henry VIII of England dissolved the smaller monasteries in his realm in 1536 and dismantled the larger ones in 1538. The crown seized all their properties, and those acts, Mr. Batham believes, drove the monks and friars of the monastic orders to band together in a secret society of mutual help and protection. His talk was later published in two parts in *The Philalethes* magazine.

I'm delighted to know that true Masonic scholars are still digging to find the truth, hampered as they are by the almost total lack of written evidence.

The principal purpose of this discourse is to call attention to a field of research so far untouched by Masonic scholars; the evidence to be found in the works of artists of the Middle Ages. Given that a secret society did exist in medieval Britain, it would be much simpler for an artist to conceal its symbolism and allegory in his paintings than for a chronicler to attempt to conceal them in his writings.

The painting reproduced on page 112 is an outstanding example of the possibilities. It is *The Wayfarer*, by the Flemish artist Hieronymus Bosch. Those familiar with Bosch's work have come to expect graphic portrayals of a wide range of hideous, distorted demons. *The Wayfarer* is different in that it depicts no demons or monsters, although it is packed with symbolism, much of it Masonic in nature.

Take a good look at the painting. The wayfarer has his left trouser leg pushed up to the knee. It might be pointed out that the trouser leg is up to accommodate a bandage, but no minor calf wound requires a slipper on one foot, with a show on the other.

The straps of the wayfarer's backpack are not over his shoulders, where they belong. Instead, Bosch has put a strap *around* his upper arms, binding him like a Masonic cable-tow. The feather we might expect to find in his hat is not there. Bosch has replaced it with a plumb bob, another Masonic symbol.

Why is the man carrying his hat in his hand, rather than conveniently wearing it on his head? Bosch may have wanted his hood ready to pull down over his face to "hoodwink" him, a word that suggests that this is the way a man was blindfolded in ancient Masonic initiation. It was a common practice at that time and was incorporated into the language for future ages in the expression "to pull the wool over his eyes."

Ahead of the traveler is a gate with a strange brace. Everyone who knows anything about wooden farm gates knows that the brace goes from one corner to the diagonally opposite corner, creating immovable triangles. The brace on Bosch's gate rises above the top rail, then comes back down to the corner. This produces a crafts-man's square on top of the gate.

Now consider the painting as a whole. The traveling man is moving from left to right, or from west to east, leaving behind him a rude, crude world. A serving maid lounges in the doorway of a decrepit tavern, holding a pitcher, while a customer kisses her, holding his hand on her breast. Around the corner, a man is urinating against the wall. In the courtyard, pigs feed at a trough, while an angry dog with a spiked collar crouches, deciding whether or not to attack.

With a few more steps the wayfarer will pass through the gate of the square and enter a land of peace and plenty, as symbolized by the placid milk cow. In the tree above his head is perched an owl, the medieval symbol for wisdom.

The final question is one of motivation. To have known the Masonic symbols before 1717 (if indeed they existed in his time), Bosch would have to have been a Masonic initiate. Is it likely that the artist would have been attracted to, and invited into, a secret society dedicated to protecting religious dissidents from the wrath of the Church? It is very probable. Bosch is known to have been a member of a religious fraternity frowned upon by the Church. His cynical portrayals of drunken, carousing monks and nuns indicate a man angry at the Church, especially in view of several condemnations of his work as heretical.

It is possible, of course, that the Masonic symbols in this painting are all merely coincidences. If so, this is the most incredible collection of Masonic coincidences that we may ever expect to see assembled in a single work. If, however, the symbols are not there coincidentally, then this painting provides the very first graphic evidence of the existence of Masonic symbolism about five hundred years ago, in the late fifteenth century. Hieronymus Bosch was born in 1450 and died in 1516. Within twelve months of his death, the great protestant religious movement in Europe was launched when the Augustinian monk, Martin Luther, nailed his Theses to the great door of the Schlosskirche in Wittenberg.

I have pointed out elsewhere the Masonic symbolism in the mural on the ceiling of the Royal Navy Hospital in Greenwich—the last building project of Sir Christopher Wren. My hope is to arouse the interest of Masons associated with the field of fine art, to the extent that they will keep one mental channel tuned to the Masonic connection whenever they examine medieval paintings, engravings, carvings, and sketches. There may well be other hidden visual evidence of Masonic existence just waiting to be spotted.

Masonic research is in many ways an unfinished temple of its own. We can only be encouraging to those Masons who approach the historical mysteries of Masonry with the conviction that the answers *must* be there *somewhere*, and wish them success. We all await that incontrovertible, documented proof that will solve the great mystery of how it all began, and why.

12

It's a Secret

OVER FIFTY YEARS ago, at about age twelve, I noticed that my Sunday school teacher was wearing a strange ring. It was a wide gold band similar to a wedding ring. What made it different was the device of an equilateral triangle with a little squiggle inside the borders. (Masons will recognize that he was wearing the ring of the 14th degree of Scottish Rite.)

Finally one Sunday, my curiosity got the better of me. I pointed to his ring and asked, "What's that?" His answer was a quick "That's a secret." "Well, what does it mean?" I asked, and with a kindly smile he cut me off: "If I told you, it wouldn't be a secret anymore, would it?"

So a group of about a dozen boys missed being told that there was such a thing as Freemasonry, and perhaps a few positive things about it. Based on what I learned years later, my Sunday school teacher could have named a dozen other men in that congregation who were also Masons. Some of us might have waited impatiently for our twenty-first birthdays, so that we might be Masons, too. And even more years later, as I learned more about Masonry, it became clear that the existence of Freemasonry and any man's membership in it were in no way "secrets." Half a century ago, some Masons apparently misunderstood the "secrets" of the lodge. Many still do.

That misunderstanding is never more destructive than in the attitudes of many Masons who fully believe that they are permitted to say nothing about Masonry to their families. I have seen letters to Masonic publications in which fathers have lamented not being allowed to tell their sons anything about the fraternity, sons whom they would very much like to join them in their lodges.

It is difficult to accept that there are many Masons who don't really understand what is secret and what is not. It is even more difficult to accept that there are men who relish having secrets in order to feel special, hoping that they will be the envy of those outside.

The latter type was brought to my attention during an autographing session at a shopping mall bookstore. A young woman asked me to sign a book for her and then said, "I hope this book will help to save my marriage!" I had to tell her that there was nothing about *Born in Blood* designed to aid marital relationships, but curiosity led me to ask her why she had made that remark.

She was twenty-three years old, her husband was twenty-five, and they had been married for seven months. He had become a Freemason soon after they returned from their honeymoon. "He says words that I don't understand," she explained, "and when I ask what they mean, he says, 'It's a secret. I can't tell you.'" There was more. "Sometimes, he stands in front of me and makes funny motions with his hands. Then when I ask him what he's doing, he says, 'It's a secret!' So I say, 'Well, if it's a secret, don't do it in front of me!'"

Having embarked on recounting her plight, her resentment poured out. "This goes on all the time. His Mason thing is driving me crazy. I wish he'd drop out of it, or stop beating on me with it." (I couldn't resist suggesting to her that she ask her husband whether *his* secrets meant that they were allowed to have secrets from each other. If he answered "Yes," as he must, she should say to him, "Oh, thank God! That makes me feel a lot better." Then, I suggested, she should let him stew for a while, wondering what *her* secrets might be, and that should serve as the basis for a truce.)

Quite apart from the fact that the young man had not matured enough to realize that teasing is not an acceptable form of humor, he was simply asserting his sense of his own importance, if not superiority. I formed a secret society with a friend when we were eight or nine years old. The society had a secret password, a secret grip, and a secret buried treasure. It also had a secret purpose, which was to annoy my kid sister. The battle cry was "I know something *you* don't know, nyah, nyah, nyah!"

There are men who have never shaken that desire to know something that others don't know. The urge can be so great that they present to themselves, and others, that they are possessed of very important hidden information or knowledge. I have even had Masonic dropouts tell me that they were disappointed because their Masonic membership had not led to their being made privy to dark secrets, which had been their sole reason for joining. That love of secrecy, even when it is totally inappropriate, can last a lifetime. I found that out one evening when I talked to an eighty-two-year-old Masonic widow.

Her husband had been a Freemason for forty-seven years when he died. From correspondence found in his desk she had learned that he was a "thirty-third degree, whatever that is," and a Knight Templar. She was annoyed because although most of their expenditures were joint efforts, "all kinds of dues" and the occasional charitable donation were completely unilateral. She was never consulted, and never got an explanation. Worst of all, he had a closet for his Masonic paraphernalia on the second floor of their home, with a lock that had just one key. She was told that if he ever failed to lock the door, she must not look inside. "I called it 'Bluebeard's Closet,'" she said.

The result, of course, was resentment. She got her revenge for his Masonic secrecy when their son, who was engaged to be married, told her that he planned to join his father's lodge. She sat him down in the kitchen for a long talk, during which she recited the feelings that his father's Masonry had engendered in her. She said, "Sweetheart, Nancy is such a lovely girl, and her happiness should be as important to you as your own. Don't do this to her, and to your marriage." Her son did not join a Masonic lodge, which she took as a personal victory. "I talked him out of it!" she said proudly.

While she was visiting our home, I asked if she would like to see a video about the Freemasons. She said she would, so I played for her *The Unseen Journey*, the sixty-minute video produced for the Grand

Lodge of Illinois. At the end she said, "I've learned more about the Masons in one hour than I did in almost fifty years of living with one. I didn't know that George Washington and all those famous men were Freemasons. And I knew nothing about all those charity projects. That's wonderful. Why didn't my husband tell me those things?"

The Mason who feels that he cannot discuss his Masonry with his wife, son, grandson, or neighbor is doing the fraternity a great disservice. The rule that no man is ever asked to become a Mason, but rather must ask to join, absolutely requires that *someone* must tell him *something* in order to establish that desire to become a Mason.

This doesn't mean that there are *no* secrets in Freemasonry, because there are. I, for one, would hate to see them abandoned. They are reminders of the days when men had to meet and identify each other in total secrecy, not as an innocent game, but as a rigid practice to protect their lives.

There is an Old Charge of Freemasonry that says that no Mason should tell the secrets of a brother Mason that can cost that brother his life and property. What secret could a medieval Mason have had that could cause such a total catastrophe? There was just one.

When Gregory IX ascended the papal throne in 1227, the Albigensian Crusade in southern France had been burning and butchering for eighteen years, without ever succeeding in wiping out the Cathar heresy. The pope decided to remove the responsibility of stamping out heresy from the secular arm and authorize the Church to undertake the purification of the faith. In 1229, he established the Inquisition, and in that same year, at the Council of Toulouse, the Church set the universal punishment for the crime of heresy. Anyone found to be a heretic, or anyone giving aid to a heretic, or anyone even giving *advice* to a heretic, merited death. In addition, the sinner's house was to be torn down, or burned down, and his land taken by the Church.

During the ensuing years, the one secret that a man could have had that would cost him his life and property was that he had material disagreement with the Church of Rome, and so could be convicted of heresy. Even treason against his king, which was punishable by death, did not incur an automatic loss of his property. The application of torture, now officially approved, meant that just to be accused of heresy could be a hideous experience, even if he was eventually judged to be innocent.

Countless men, no doubt, went into permanent hiding. Others banded together to help each other, as did the Lollards in England and various groups on the Continent. Examination of the Old Charges of Masonry that define the assistance to be given a brother away from home indicate very clearly that Freemasonry was one of these groups. And the only way any such group could survive and function effectively was as a secret society.

When revealing oneself could bring such physical and economic tragedy, any man can be expected to demand all the protection from betrayal that he can get. That is why candidates for membership in the society were blindfolded until they had taken their oaths to keep their brothers' secrets. Only then were they permitted to see the faces of the other men in the room.

Since even to be spotted attending a clandestine meeting might mean betrayal and death, a lookout or sentry was always posted when members gathered. Freemasons remember that function with the lodge officer called the Tyler, who stands guard outside the meeting room in a purely symbolic role. At one time the Tyler stood at his post with a drawn sword in his hand. Now he is more likely to be sitting, and his sword of office is often a three-inch replica hanging as a pendant on a chain around his neck. The Tyler's services as a guard are no longer critical for the safety of the men attending the meeting. But his office does serve to remind his Masonic brothers of the time when such security *was* a vital necessity, and to remind them to remember and honor their predecessors who risked their lives in the struggle for religious freedom.

The risks encountered by those medieval Masons in their daily lives were as great as those in the lodge meetings. To help a brother on the run from the threat of torture and death, it was essential to have a system of words and signs of recognition that could be used wherever the Mason might find himself. There were terms, phrases, and questions that could be worked into ordinary conversation so that a fellow Mason would recognize a brother in need. A seemingly innocent response would tell the man needing help that he had made the right contact. There were signs of recognition and handgrips that could be used without any words spoken, for mutual recognition and the promise of shelter, food, or guidance.

These are the catechisms, hand signals, and handgrips that are preserved today, even though they are no longer needed. Today, Freemasons can be recognized as such by means of decals, bumper stickers, and baseball caps, not to mention dues cards in their wallets. So why do they cling to those "secrets"? For the same reason that we celebrate Veterans' Day, Memorial Day, and Presidents' Day; for the same reason we reenact Civil War battles and teach our children the dying words of Nathan Hale and battle cries like "Remember the Alamo!" There are traditions worth preserving and men worth remembering. The Masonic "secrets" help a fraternity to remember men who took terrible risks to help gain those personal freedoms which we believe all men are entitled to enjoy.

Yes, some will say, but why do the Freemasons have to maintain their traditions in total secrecy? The answer is that they don't. Non-Masons have known the "secret" words and signals for over two and a half centuries and still enjoy "revealing" them. What the anti-Masons miss is the overridingly important point that Masons never change their "secrets," however many times they are revealed. Think about that!

If a battlefield commander even suspects that his password has leaked to the enemy, he immediately changes the password. In a truly secret organization, the revelation of a secret term, a recognition or distress signal, necessitates a prompt change because the secret signs are protecting secret information. They are not symbolic, as they are in Freemasonry, but tools of subversion. The "secrets" in Freemasonry appear in articles, pamphlets, radio shows, books, and videotapes; yet they are never changed by so much as a syllable or gesture.

The Masons do not change those well-known secret signs, passwords, and recognition signals because their uses, in their traditional forms, are "rites of remembrance." They well know that all of their traditional secrets are no longer secret.

A comparable situation may be found in some tours of the "stately homes" of England, in which tourists are shown secret "priest-holes." These were secret rooms or compartments where loyal Catholics hid their priests from the "Pursuivants," the royal priest-catchers eager to escort them to the headsman's block. They are no longer secret, and they are no longer needed. Yet they are carefully preserved as a reminder of how dangerous life and religious faith used to be.

In addition to their condemnations of Masonic recognition signals, anti-Masons also find evil in the fact that only a Mason in good standing can attend a lodge meeting. They ask, "Why do Masons need secret meetings?" In fact, notices of those meetings, giving the place, date, and time, frequently appear in highly visible places, like local newspapers, hardly appropriate for a truly clandestine gathering. Masonic meetings are not secret, they are simply for paid-up members only, hardly an unusual feature.

Sometimes private lodge meetings deal with matters that *should* be confidential. They may consider giving assistance to a brother's widow, handle criticism of a member from within or from outside the lodge, consider chastisement of a member who appears to have behaved in a manner that falls short of the moral standards expected of a Mason. It is proper that this sort of membership business should not be carried out in public.

The vibrant Masonic world isn't secret at all. Masonic history is freely available to all. Masonic beliefs and principles are never secret and can be easily discovered by anyone interested. Ten-dollar books, sold by television evangelists and purporting to contain dark Masonic secrets, actually reveal nothing that isn't available at no charge whatsoever at any good public library (naturally, they keep *that* fact a *real* secret). When they lie, as they frequently do, that information is, of course, available only in their sensational books.

The best protection against allegations of secret worship, secret plots, and subversion of religion is to make known to the world just what Freemasonry is all about. The fraternity must stop hiding its light under a bushel. Lack of knowledge creates a void that is amply filled by anti-Masons with half-truths, perverted truths, and outright falsehoods that appeal to a natural human weakness, a taste for scandal. Ignorance is the real enemy.

Many Masons are poorly informed right at the beginning. Some are so exhilarated by learning "secrets" that they don't know where those secrets stop. More than once I have observed two Masons loading their conversation with Masonic terms, clearly to impress a non-Mason present. The truth is that a non-Mason is much more likely to be irritated than impressed by such a demonstration.

If I seem to be going overboard with my criticism of the handling and misunderstanding of Masonic secrets, consider this example of misdirected secrecy and its counterproductive result:

While waiting for a show to begin, I was sitting in the lounge, talking to the talk-show host. He related an experience he had had earlier that day, while picking up his car from the service department of an import car dealer. The owner approached him and said, "I heard the announcement that you'll be talking about the Masons tonight. I'll be listening." "Why?" the host asked, "Are you a Free-mason?" "No," the dealer replied, "but my best friend is. We talked about it on a fishing trip a couple of weeks ago."

It seemed the dealer's friend had suggested that he was the kind of man the Masons want and that it would be fun for them to be Masons together in the same lodge. In the ensuing conversation, the dealer tried to find out something – anything – about Masonry, to help him decide whether or not he wanted to become one. The Masonic friend would tell him nothing and finally said, "Look, once you take the oath and you're in, we'll tell you everything you want to know." "What is the oath about?" the dealer asked. His friend said that as he took part in the initiation, the oath would be revealed to him. "You mean that I'm supposed to swear an oath, but I won't know what I'm swearing to until later?" His friend replied, "Something like that." "Forget it!" said the dealer. "Let's just fish."

He did not become a Mason, and the reason is no secret.

13

"Don't Talk to Me about Change!"

B Y NO MEANS do all Masons agree with all the actions of their
brothers or their leaders.

One of the strongest disagreements among Masons today
is the matter of change. Some feel a definite need to change aspects of
Masonic custom, to conform better to current society. Others feel that
any variation in tradition, custom, or ritual would be almost sacri-
legious. Some of those in favor of change want to take steps more
drastic than do others.

So there are two problems here: whether or not there should be
any changes whatsoever, and how serious those changes should be.
Then, of course, there is the disagreement as to just what it is that
should change, and what should remain inviolate. In a sense, the
latter point is the heart of the matter. All want to do what is
right, and doing the right thing is easy. On the other hand, deciding
what the right thing *is* can be difficult, stressful, and controversial.

Contemplating the whole matter is difficult, too, because in the
Masonic fraternity in America the final authority is distributed geo-
graphically among fifty-one Grand Lodges. What one Grand Lodge
accepts can be totally rejected by the others.

Generally, each Grand Lodge recognizes the others' jurisdictional authority, and in spite of differences they can go forward in the spirit of brotherhood, which is the essence of the Masonic philosophy. Yet if one Grand Lodge is angry with another, in the belief that some action taken violates inviolable tradition, that angry Grand Lodge can abandon all recognition of and fellowship with the other — as has happened on several occasions.

One point at issue is the rule that no man is ever invited to become a Mason but must make that decision on his own, then petition a lodge for admission. That position, say some, coupled with many Masons' belief that they may not discuss Masonry with any outsider, puts a definite brake on new memberships. One solution suggested would make it possible for Masons to extend an invitation to members of their immediate families, such as sons, grandsons, and brothers. (Some Grand Lodges around the world, however, have the exact opposite practice, in that no man can ask to be a Freemason, but each must wait to be invited.) Another course would be to correct by education the misimpression that there is nothing meaningful about Masonry that a Freemason can impart to a non-member.

For those who feel that no change whatsoever can be tolerated, consideration might be given to this: In 1717, only four lodges in London came out into the light of public view. A year earlier, in 1716, all the lodges in England, Scotland, Ireland, and Wales were part of a secret society whose very existence was virtually unknown. How did those lodges gain new members over the centuries? How did men work up a strong desire to join an organization of whose existence they were totally unaware? Reason says that the only way that a man could have become a Mason in those days was by being *asked* to be one. I am not speaking in favor of changing the present regulation. Rather, I am merely suggesting that it cannot possibly have its roots in ancient Masonic tradition. When the present rule was made, it was a *change* from ancient tradition.

So it is with many aspects of Freemasonry today. When Masonry became public, there were only two degrees, the Entrant and the Fellow. A fellow is a peer, an equal, a full member. The only masters were the masters of the lodges. Then, somewhere along the line, a group of leaders decided that it would be well if every Mason could be a Master. Besides, that title suited the growing preoccupation with tracing the ancestry of Freemasonry to guilds of stonemasons. A full member of a guild was called a master, so they changed the degree work and designation to accommodate the guild concept and instituted the degree of Master Mason. That was a *change*.

Originally, in 1717, there were no moral lessons taught with masons' tools. Those, too, were incorporated later, and as part of the dedication to the medieval guild origin theory. Each one of those things constituted a *change*.

Much better known is the regulation banning alcoholic beverages from the symbolic lodge. It is probably a good rule, but there can hardly be any doubt that it is in direct opposition to the customs of the ancient lodges, which usually met in the upper rooms of taverns. At first, they drank the products of the tavern during the course of the meetings, smoking their pipes as well. Only later were smoking and drinking removed from the lodge meeting and confined to the later period of refreshment. And only much, much later did the American lodges vote to keep alcohol out of the lodge completely. That regulation, strictly enforced today, was a very dramatic *change*.

The point of all this is that Freemasonry has always adapted, adjusted, and changed, a fact which is at least partially responsible for its longevity. The genius of the U.S. Constitution was that it carefully spelled out the means by which it could be altered, added to, or subtracted from, according to the needs of succeeding generations. Had it been unalterably, unchangeably rigid, it probably would have cracked apart years ago.

Given that, it becomes important to emphasize that significant changes should not be lightly adopted. Sometimes change appears to be the only answer to fear, or to criticism. Any change requires cool consideration and careful examination. (Not, however, as cool and careful as the Vatican, which upon finally receiving the report of a special committee at work for thirteen years decided, in 1992, that Galileo had not been guilty of heresy 359 years earlier. That's a bit slow.)

For example, take the problem of men who become Masonic Entered Apprentices, then drop out of the fraternity without ever taking the next step. I know of no available figures, but based on the numbers given to me by several Grand Lodges, I will venture a guess that at least two hundred thousand men in the United States completed just the first degree, then dropped out. Obviously, some adjustment is called for, but what?

I am not aware of any survey that has been taken to ascertain the precise reasons for the withdrawals, but there is no shortage of theories. One is that some men were offended by the penalty of the obligation. Another is that the men had expected to learn some truly esoteric secrets but weren't taught any. By far the most prevalent cause suggested is the requirement for extensive memorizing, not just because some lack talent for memorizing, but because the subsequent examination takes place before the entire lodge, which can be embarrassing to the point of humiliation.

One Grand Lodge has already done away with the memorization, on the basis that the simple act of recitation does not mean that the candidate truly understands what he is reciting. Instead, that Grand Lodge has instituted a program of four seminars which the new man must attend. The groups are small and private, with the emphasis on understanding. The most unusual feature of this innovation is that the man being instructed has the option of bringing his wife to the fourth seminar, which covers Masonic history and current activities. It is believed, sensibly, to be beneficial that a man's wife, right at the beginning of her husband's Masonic career, be given the opportunity to learn what Masonry is all about and to ask her own questions.

Another Grand Lodge is considering changing the examination from a formal function, with the man standing before the whole lodge, to a private, informal examination by a committee of three. This would help the initiate to relax, especially by removing the stress created through having every tiny error put on public display.

As to the penalties of the obligations, some jurisdictions have simply eliminated them from the initiation. I cannot fully favor that course, because I feel that this part of the ritual acts as a reminder of those earlier Masons who risked their lives and property to belong to the fraternity. The penalties are mild punishment compared to the legal agonies that could be inflicted on any Mason in the fourteenth, fifteenth, and sixteenth centuries who was betrayed by having his dedication to religious freedom exposed. Some Masons feel that the penalties should be removed from the oath but recited separately, to preserve an ancient tradition – a sort of "lest we forget."

Whatever is or isn't done, it seems clear that the initiate should have emphasized to him that no Mason is ever called upon to inflict those penalties: They are symbolic of a bygone age. Since no one is designated to inflict the penalties, it seems that God is being called upon to perform them, much as we might say "Cross my heart and hope to die" or "May God strike me down with a bolt of lightning if I am not telling the truth" to affirm our sincerity.

Another change being discussed as a result of declining membership and a decline in attendance at lodge meetings is the nature of those meetings. Some feel that their lodges meet too frequently, making unnecessary time demands on their members. Certainly, American lodges meet more frequently than those in England and other countries, perhaps in response to social conditions that prevailed a few generations ago, before television and movies, when there was precious little to do in the evenings in many towns across the country. Now a wide variety of events, entertainments, and family obligations tend to make any function a demand on a busy time schedule. Most Grand Lodges have taken no action at all, but one Grand Master ruled that the lodges in his state should meet no more than six times a year. One of the justifications for such a move was that it would be a lot easier to arrange interesting programs for six meetings than for twelve or twenty.

As a carry-over from the days of a farming economy, when most farm families only came to town on market day, there are still some lodges that meet on Saturday evening. That certainly does not meet with the enthusiastic approval of wives, who do not enjoy sitting home alone on Saturday nights in their marital state any more than they did when they were single.

Dress code has become an issue in some areas, where certain members feel that a lodge meeting merits a level of respect that should be reflected in the way the members dress. Many favor a dress code of jacket and tie, believing that the atmosphere and formality of the lodge room is violated when a member ties his Masonic apron around blue jeans and a Hawaiian sport shirt.

Whatever changes may be proposed and argued over concerning the conduct of the meetings of individual lodges, those arguments certainly indicate the concern of the membership. Most Masons seem to be aware that meetings need to be more vibrant and interesting to increase the present level of attendance, which is running at less than 10 percent of paid-up members.

In my opinion, one of the barriers to constructive action lies in the structure of Grand Lodge administration. For a period of years a man works his way up through the line of Grand Lodge offices, until the time arrives when he becomes the Grand Master—the supreme authority for his Masonic jurisdiction. In most Grand Lodges the Grand Master has just twelve months to implement the plans he has spent several years thinking about, while he waited for his turn at supreme authority.

Unfortunately, the system that has evolved lays booby traps that will materially impede his ability to get everything done in that one short year. On arriving at the topmost position, he becomes the figurehead of his jurisdiction, called upon frequently to represent his Grand Lodge at a wide variety of functions, to bestow and receive honors, and to attend Masonic funeral services, along with a host of other time-consuming activities that have little to do with the administration of his Grand Lodge.

In Ohio, where I live, there are twenty-six Masonic districts, so the Grand Master is expected to drive back and forth across the state to attend, and address, twenty-six Grand Officer receptions. His wife is expected to accompany him to those formal banquets, so a good part of her weekends that year are taken up by packing and unpacking and checking in and out of motels.

The newly installed Grand Master is also expected to attend major Scottish Rite, York Rite, and Shrine functions in his jurisdiction, and to be present at functions of the Grand Lodges in nearby states. (For one Grand Master I talked to recently, every single weekend of his year, except for Christmas, will be taken up by a Masonic occasion.)

Such a grueling schedule inevitably impairs any Grand Master's ability to administer his jurisdiction and to implement the programs that he feels will benefit the Craft. And whatever he achieves, it is with the full knowledge that in a few months his successor may well set aside everything he has done, in order to implement projects of his own.

To an outsider, one of the most distressing aspects of this administrative system is what happens to a Grand Master after his one year is up. He spends years in a succession of posts, gaining knowledge and experience, until his efforts culminate in his being installed as Grand Master—the pinnacle of his success and power. As soon as his term expires, he drops from any real position of authority. Thus the Grand Lodge system might be likened to a man making a slow climb up a mountainside. When he reaches the top, he does not climb back down, but is pushed off the cliff. Most of us could agree that with experience comes knowledge, and that the two together produce judgment, the greatest attribute of true leadership. Thus the role of the Past Grand Master may represent a great waste of talent.

One way around that waste might be to create a five-man board of governors made up of the five most recent Past Grand Masters, with the immediate Past Grand Master as its chairman. Now five men of recent experience and sound judgment would have a role in Grand Lodge direction and supervision. The Grand Master would still be the chief executive officer, much as a corporation president runs a company with direct authority, but within guidelines and budgets set by a board of directors.

This plan, of course, requires the current Grand Master to give up a little authority. On the other hand, if he feels somewhat cramped by the board as Grand Master, he can always look forward to being chairman of that board for a year after his term of office ends, when he will be in a position to influence the continuance of the programs he put in place. His overriding satisfaction should come from the fact that he is not going to be summarily dumped a few months from now, but will have an influence on the affairs of his Grand Lodge for the next five years. That would be a major change!

In summary, scientists studying the development of species and trying to discover why so many have become extinct have concluded that intelligence can be defined as *adaptability*. Those groups that have adapted have survived and grown. That applies to governments, religions, and primitive tribes (which we all once were). At a crucial point in its life, the Catholic Church lost tens of millions of members because it delayed too long in adaptation and adjustment. Governments and religious denominations today are struggling to adapt all over the world, agonizing over what should change and what must remain the same.

Many Freemasons are distressed by the decline in membership, although the current base of two and a half million men in this country alone is strong enough to weather some storms, as it has done before. It would be easier to address the decline if it was for a specific reason, such as the Morgan affair and the anti-Masonic political party of the past century, when the Masons were accused (but not found guilty) of the murder of a defected member. Those problems were clearly understood. Today's problems are more difficult to pinpoint.

No one claims a comprehensive knowledge and understanding of the forces at work now, because they are not confined to Masonry. All secular fraternal societies are in a state of decline. Of all the religious groups in the United States, only the fundamentalists' numbers are increasing, perhaps because they offer their adherents total freedom from the stress of having to think things through for themselves. The Catholic Church appears to be holding its own only because of the great waves of Catholic Hispanic immigrants. The shortage of priests is critical. Catholic schools, academies, monasteries, and convents have closed in discouraging numbers.

Pessimists see all this as a sign of a decline in public morality, a decline that makes any organization that insists on high standards of moral conduct unpopular. Others feel that the abundance of entertainment and leisure-time activities—especially television—have become more attractive than active participation in any church or fraternal society.

On a personal front, I recall the time when the preparation of the evening meal was the biggest family event of my mother's day. She started at two or three o'clock in the afternoon. There were roasts, pies, cakes, even the occasional homemade bread. I would have rather eaten at home than in any restaurant. But then we acquired a television set. My aging mother got hooked on soap operas. Now preparing dinner became a last-minute, scurrying, slam-bang affair. Prepackaged foods and canned vegetables became the order of the day, with dessert served quickly after removing the plastic wrapper from supermarket pastries.

After dinner, the family no longer sat around and talked, read books, or took long walks. Instead, the living-room furniture was rearranged so that everyone could get a good head-on look at the box, which we all stared at through the eleven o'clock news. Later, with the advent of color cartoons, the TV became the electronic baby-sitter. The kids could be kept quiet if they were entertained. My family's experience was multiplied millions of times over wherever television sets were sold. What began as a luxury item became an absolute necessity, even for the poverty-stricken.

Who can measure how it changed our lives? We became the most entertained society in the world. And as standards of living rose, most families managed to have two cars, and children who used to walk or ride their bikes now had to be chauffeured everywhere. An economy that had produced a greater array of labor-saving devices than at any other time in history suddenly found that society saying, "We just don't have the time."

Clearly, Freemasonry must present a purpose. It must offer activities that will give it a status that warrants taking a little time away from other pursuits. Some might point out, correctly, that everything that's needed is already there, but no one knows anything about it. How can the unknown be appealing? A good part of the answer may lie in an organized effort to get the word out.

The men of today that Freemasonry is looking for appear to be concerned about their families, their professional careers, and their physical fitness. If true, no one can fault them for those concerns. How can Masonry relate to them?

Any number of young men have told me of their decision not to become Masons, based on a complete misunderstanding of the fraternity. "They try to tell you how to run your life." "It's all just ritual." "They don't *do* anything." "It looks to me like it's a goody-two-shoes group of old men." "It's not macho—you know, *manly*." It is time for some of that Masonic education activity that exists in every Grand Lodge to be directed toward the general public.

In all this discussion of change-or-no-change, Freemasonry has one great advantage. With over thirteen thousand lodges, a new idea can be tried with just a few of them, to be tested before it is introduced on a broad scale. The problem now is this: If a small group does discover a successful new idea for increasing lodge meeting attendance, for more fruitful Masonic friendship programs and so on, how can that good idea be spread throughout the fraternity nationwide so that others can use it? With fifty-one separate jurisdictions, it's entirely possible for one Grand Lodge to come up with a brilliant plan that really works but have it remain virtually unknown to the other fifty.

The fastest answer I see to that problem can be found in the Masonic Service Association. The staff is eager to distribute helpful information, and I'm certain that they would welcome contributions to a program that might be called the Masonic Idea File. They would print up successful ideas and distribute a letter or pamphlet, always giving full credit to the sources.

There are two things of which we can be certain. First, changes *will* come. They are already appearing in individual Grand Lodges. Second, there will be Masons who will be angered and will denounce those changes vehemently as violations of ancient tradition. As that happens, we can only ask those proposing or making such changes to respect the dissidents' devotion to custom and tradition. For those defending the history and traditions of Freemasonry, we can point to the fact that a good part of that history gives evidence of a great number of changes throughout the centuries.

14

A Masonic Idea File

I N THE WORLD of sales promotion, sales management, advertising, and public relations in which I spent my early years in business, there was a constant call for creativity, for fresh ideas and concepts. One of the means devised to stimulate that creative thinking was called "brainstorming."

The big difference between Brainstorming and Think Tank was that in a brainstorming session all thoughts were positive. Any negative reaction to an idea or proposal was stopped by the chairman with a bell or whistle. There were a couple of sound reasons for this approach. One was that not all creative people are strongly assertive by nature, and too often an argument can be won by forceful oratory, or the exercise of authority, rather than by logic. The victim of such a put-down often retreats within himself and his thoughts are lost to the group. The other reason was that in any group there are people whose immediate response to every idea is negative. They compensate for their own fear of appearing uncreative by finding fault with the contributions of others— even though they may come around later, and then indignantly deny having tried earlier to discredit their colleagues' efforts.

There were, of course, frequently very valid and logical reasons for objecting to a proposal, but these were squelched, too, to ensure the free flow of ideas. The big point here is that an idea might be too expensive to implement, too wild, or unsuitable for other reasons, but there was always the possibility that it would serve as a stimulant for imaginative thinking within the group that could, eventually, give rise to a concept both original and practical.

That is the spirit in which I am presenting here a few ideas of my own. They may not be suitable for the Masonic bodies they are designed to help, but they will, I hope, stimulate creative thinking in others closer to the situation. If they accomplish no more than that I shall be happy.

To begin, my experience tells me that Freemasonry is virtually unknown on most college campuses, even though Masonic bodies fund many scholarships every year. Why not shed a little local light on this activity? Advertising is generally offered at a low rate in college and university newspapers. My thought is that for each scholarship awarded an announcement ad should be purchased, perhaps four or five times the size of a business card. Its function would include honoring the recipient. Recognition must be given to the fact that the public does not quickly associate every Masonic body with Freemasonry, so the ad should do that for them. For example, the wording might be:

THE FREEMASONS OF PENNSYLVANIA CONGRATULATE
Kathleen M. Winslow
WHOSE ACHIEVEMENTS HAVE EARNED FOR HER A
SCHOLARSHIP AWARDED BY
THE SCOTTISH RITE VALLEY OF PITTSBURGH
SCHOLARSHIP FUND

Freemasonry in general and the contributing body in particular are both recognized. If a graphic square and compasses could be in the ad, so much the better, just to start building a favorable image.

Ms. Winslow will have been honored, and every student on that campus will be made aware of the fact that there are such people as Freemasons and that they support higher education. In all likelihood the Valley will receive some calls from students asking for information about scholarship applications.

Obviously, it is very desirable to make contact with young people years before they reach college age; and something *can* be done about that. It must start inside the lodge, with the Masons themselves.

In response to my questions to Masons as to why they had not told their sons and grandsons about Masonry, I was frequently told, "They're just not interested," and, "I don't know how to introduce the subject." This suggestion is an attempt to relieve those problems. Age eighteen is a bit late, since a young man of that age has a variety of other things on his mind. Even the middle teens may be a bit late, since it is the time of initial discovery that there is an opposite sex and of the all-important countdown to the birthday that permits the youngster to apply for a driver's license. I suggest that age twelve is the time to reveal Masonry to him, and in a most dramatic manner.

The lodge would designate one annual stated meeting after which the lodge would receive and honor any sons and grandsons of members who had reached age twelve that year. For simplicity, let's assume that one father brings one son, timing his arrival to coincide with the regular closing. It is extremely important to try to envision the following scene from the viewpoint of a twelve-year-old boy, to whom the ceremony will be new and mysterious.

The father introduces the Tyler, who immediately informs someone inside of their arrival. When ready, the Tyler raps on the door and the father and son are met and led (don't grip the boy by the upper arm!) to the Worshipful Master.

> **W.M.:** Welcome, brother Miller. Who is this young man whom you have brought with you this evening into the ancient precincts of the Masonic lodge?

> **Father:** W.M., this is my son, David. He is good at school and loves soccer and swimming. He is very helpful to his mother in the house and to me outside. We are very proud of him, and I wanted him to meet some of my Masonic brothers.

> **W.M.:** David, you are very welcome here. We are all your father's Masonic brothers. Please sit here.
> David, this must seem a strange room to you. Everything in it has a meaning, even including the

arrangement of the chairs, all of which will be explained to you if, after you have reached the age of twenty-one, you decide to follow your father into Freemasonry.

In the meantime, there are two things in this room that are very familiar to you: The Holy Bible is here, because every Freemason believes in God. Our country's flag is here, because every Freemason loves his country. Many Masons have fought and died for it.

In their devotion to God, Freemasons believe that every important event should begin by asking the blessing of our Creator, which we shall do now.

SUGGESTED INVOCATION:

Dear heavenly father, we are meeting here tonight to honor David Miller, son of our respected brother, Charles Miller. A long full life is ahead of David, and we ask that you bless him with good health and assist him in his endeavors, as he works to gain an education and goes out into the world to seek his furtune. He is soon to be a man. Help him to be a good man, and a happy man. Amen.

All: So mote it be.

W.M.: And now, David, it is our custom to honor our nation's flag.

PLEDGE OF ALLEGIANCE

David, we in this room are just a tiny part of your father's Masonic brothers around the world. There are five million of us in all, in a fraternity that goes back before the founding of our country, and before Columbus discovered America. You hear about many of those Masons in your history lessons at school. Let us give a few examples. Brother _____, please read for David a list of his father's Masonic brothers who have served as presidents of the United States.

Br_____: David, here are your father's Masonic brothers who served as presidents of the United States: [*Reads list*]

W.M.: Thank you, Brother_____. David, we know that you have studied the history of our country in school and know of the many heroes who took part in it. You may not know that many of those heroes in our nation's history were your father's Masonic brothers. Brother_____, please read for David a list of just a few of his father's Masonic brothers who helped to found and preserve this nation.

Br_____: David, these are just a very few of the heroes in American history who were proud to be Freemasons, starting with the American Revolution right up to the space programs: [*Reads brief list, starting with Washington, Franklin, and Paul Revere, ending with Buzz Aldrin*]

W.M.: Thank you, Brother_____. There is a great deal more that can be learned about Freemasonry, David: about hospitals for young children, homes for the elderly, and all manner of Masonic charities. We won't take your time to talk about them this evening, but if you want to know more, just talk to your father. He'll be happy to tell you about them.

As you look around at the men in this room, bear in mind that every man here is with your father in Masonic brotherhood. Just as any one of them would help your father, so any of them will help you, if ever you need it.

That ends the serious part of our evening together. We thank you for coming, because your father talks about you, and we were eager to meet you. After the meeting we will have some refreshments, and we have a gift for you.

Just as we opened this meeting with a prayer, we close every meeting with a benediction.

[*Calls for benediction*] So mote it be.

At refreshments, present the boy with a gift. My suggestion is a baseball cap with square and compasses, because that won't get tacked to the wall of his room. The whole evening's events should not take more than thirty to forty-five minutes: quite long enough for a twelve-year-old.

That boy will go home and tell his mother, brothers, and sisters what he experienced that night. And what will he talk about to all his friends at school the next day? In terms of membership, he won't even be eligible to apply for membership for nine more years, but there should be more immediate benefits. He will no longer be puzzled by or feel left out of a part of his father's life. As to the fatherly complaint about the subject of Masonry expressed in "I don't know how to bring it up," that problem is gone. Chances are rather good that his son will bring it up. And when the boy hears that Dad is going to a lodge meeting tonight, he knows very well where his father is going. He'll feel special.

There's another way to broaden that family awareness of Masonry, which I first mentioned in a 1992 Grand Masters' workshop. Several men have since told me that they have tried it and it works, so I'll pass it along here.

Considering the wide variety of Masonic charities, and their success, it seems reasonable to assume that many Freemasons make charitable contributions from time to time. When they do, it is probably a personal matter. They simply write their checks and send them in. What I'm suggesting is that to do it that way is to waste a wonderful opportunity to involve the whole family, by making them all part of the act of compassion.

It's a simple plan. At some family gathering, such as Sunday dinner, bring up the problem to everyone, kids and all: "There are badly crippled little children who need help. There are children who need help to learn how to read and write. There are elderly people who cannot afford the surgery they need to keep from going blind." Say to the family, "I think we should help. What do you think?" It's difficult to imagine a negative response.

When the check is sent, accompany it with a letter that says something like this (without the italics):

> The McCormick *family* believes that you are doing wonderful work in helping those in need, and *we* would like to help. Enclosed is *our* check for fifty dollars. *We* wish you the best of success in your endeavors.

The letter should be followed by lines for the signatures of *every* member of the family old enough to write. The extra cost is nothing, and now your entire family is involved in a Masonic activity. As a side benefit, children learn about caring and giving at a very early age. (And if your children are all grown, include your grandchildren.)

One Mason who tried the idea told me that he was startled at the reaction, especially from his nine-year-old daughter. He said, "She told the woman next door, her school teacher, her Sunday school teacher . . . just anyone who would listen!" She thought more of herself, and more of her father. What a great reward for such a small effort!

The reason for these suggestions about greater family involvement is the surprising number of conversations I have had indicating the lack of information, or the misinformation, which confuses family members. Some are just curious, but others are resentful. One young woman said, "My father was a Mason for all of his life, but he never told Mama or me *anything*. What is it?" A young man said, "I asked [my father] about it, and he told me that he couldn't tell me anything. So what? I don't tell him everything about *my* life, either." (And what are the chances that *that* young man will ever become a Mason?) One woman complained, "Every time one of us does something alone, we tell each other about it, *except* when he goes to a Masonic meeting. Then suddenly it's none of my business."

Does *every* married Mason's wife feel that way? Of course not. In any group of two and a half million men there is bound to be an endless variety of personalities and family behavior. Many Masons include their wives whenever they can, and well over a million wives, daughters, mothers, and sisters of Master Masons have joined the related Order of the Eastern Star. But it is an area that hundreds of conversations have made clear leaves substantial room for improvement.

First of all, when a Mason first enters the lodge he should tell his wife and older children what Freemasonry is, and what it stands for. I am not alone in believing this, and some plans have been launched to solve the problem. One Grand Lodge sends a letter to the wife of every new married Entered Apprentice. Another gives a program on the history of Masonry, to which a new Mason is invited to bring his wife. Those efforts, although praiseworthy, are scattered, and affect only a small percentage of Masonic families across the country.

The seminar, or meeting, seems to be the most effective way to tell wives about Masonry, especially when the program is arranged to encourage the wives to ask questions. Since new men seldom enter more than one or two at a time, perhaps that meeting should be an annual event. In the meantime, there is something that can be done on the very night he becomes an Entered Apprentice.

My suggestion is an inexpensive card, setting forth the basic principles of Masonry, to be taken home to show to the new member's family, his minister, and any friends who express interest.

I envision a folding card like a standard horizontal greeting card. (It should be available for pennies, if bought in quantity.) On the outside would appear the Square and Compasses, with a line for the man's name, and followed by a message, such as:

CONGRATULATIONS TO

_____

WHO HAS JOINED THE ANCIENT ORDER OF FREEMASONS
AND HAS ACCEPTED THE PRINCIPLES SET FORTH HEREIN.

(The suggested language inside is no more than just that. It will need to be revised and edited to meet the needs of the individual Grand Lodge. It might run something like this:)

BASIC MASONIC PRINCIPLES

- Every Freemason asserts his belief in God, and in the immortality of the soul.

- A Freemason believes that how he worships God is his own business, and how every other Mason worships God is *his* own business. Accordingly, Masons believe fervently in freedom of religion.

- Freemasonry offers no pathway to salvation. That must be sought and found in a Mason's own place of worship, which he is encouraged to attend and to support.

- Because religion and politics are so often used to drive men apart, they may not be discussed in any Masonic lodge.

- Freemasonry seeks to give men of all creeds a way to meet in brotherhood and mutual respect, to join together in common causes to benefit those in need.

- If a Mason's own religious beliefs require of him a voluntary life of caring and sharing, of attention to the needs of the less fortunate, Freemasonry offers a variety of charitable outlets to satisfy his compassion. To that extent, Masonry strives to be the ideal partner of any moral religion.

- A Mason must never put his duties and responsibilities to Masonry ahead of his duties and responsibilities to his family, to his God, or to his country.

Extra copies should be readily available, in the event that the new Freemason would like to give a separate one to his family, or minister, or any non-Masonic friend who has expressed curiosity and interest. The card contains no point that he cannot discuss in more detail, should anyone wish to know more.

Best of all, everything required by this program can be handled by the lodge secretary. The lodge needs to become more involved in every way in the problem-solving process, because it is the root of all Masonic activity.

I have more thoughts about Masonry at the symbolic lodge level which, because of the importance of the symbolic lodge, deserve a separate discussion.

15

The Roots of All Masonry

ANUMBER OF SHRINERS have complained to me about the decline in York Rite and Scottish Rite membership. The Shrine must draw all of its new members from the ranks of 32nd degree Scottish Rite Masons and York Rite Knights Templar. When the membership in York Rite and Scottish Rite declines, the number of Shriners must also decline, through what the critics see as no fault of their own.

On the other hand, York Rite and Scottish Rite must draw all of their new members from the Master Masons of the symbolic lodges. When lodge membership declines, it follows that York Rite and Scottish Rite membership must also decline.

It would seem, then, to be in the interest of all Masonic bodies to look to the health and the fate of the neighborhood symbolic lodges. There certainly is a movement in that direction, but as yet no really effective form of assistance has been found.

There are a number of elements to be considered, and the first is attitude. The official attitude is that a member can achieve no status higher than the ancient third degree, that of Master Mason, which he reaches in his local lodge. He is told emphatically that there are no higher degrees. It is difficult to imagine anyone fully comprehending the basis on which the fourth degree is not higher than the third, and the 32nd degree not stratospherically higher than that. The basis for the contention is that symbolic lodge Masonry was born in forgotten antiquity, while all other Masonic systems are relatively modern, with their origins well known.

There is an attempt to keep the old tradition alive by never, ever referring to any newer Masonic system as constituting a "higher" degree; the other systems are referred to as "appendant" Masonic bodies. The idea is that after a man becomes a Master Mason he can go no *higher* in Masonry, although he can certainly move a considerable distance sideways. In practice, however, I have heard many Masons refer to their "higher degrees," with the conviction that that is exactly what they are.

One evening, a very bright young man who had achieved a high office in York Rite explained to me the problems he encountered with local lodges. "Some of those men," he told me, "get hung up on the importance of their symbolic lodges and are happy to stay Master Masons. I try to explain to them that the local lodge is like boot camp. It's like elementary school. You should get that behind you as soon as possible and move on to the 'university level' of York Rite or Scottish Rite." He certainly does not believe that the degree of Master Mason is as high as a man can get.

One great advantage of the appendant degrees is a concentration of funds and authority. There is just one Scottish Rite Valley or Shrine Temple in each city. They have a central treasury and paid full-time administrators. Generally, they have much loftier buildings and stage more elaborate events than can any one of what may be several dozen local lodges in the same cities. When a Master Mason enters an appendant body he meets other Masons from all parts of his community. There is a great appeal to devote his time and attention to that body, often to the total neglect of his own lodge, whose meetings are neither as large nor as ceremonial.

That certainly must be one contributing factor to the severe decline in attendance at local lodge meetings. Grand Lodge officers I have talked with recently indicate that only 8 or 9 percent of the total membership of a lodge attend its regular meetings. Many would probably drop out altogether, if the appendant systems did not have a rule that their members must maintain an "active member" status in their lodges as a condition of membership in the appendant systems. An "active member" is defined as one who mails his dues to his lodge every year. He need take no part in the activities of that lodge.

This situation calls to mind a conversation with a minister about "Christmas Christians," those who attend just one church service during the whole year. The minister had concluded that while he would much prefer regular attendance, he would rather see a member once a year than never see him in church at all. Perhaps that could do as a starting goal for Masons. Attend just one lodge meeting each year.

I don't believe that there is any hope of ever enforcing annual attendance as a rule, but perhaps the matter could be approached as an appeal that the members attend a meeting set up for just that purpose. For discussion, let's consider an arrangement between a Grand Lodge and all the Scottish Rite Valleys within its jurisdiction.

The Grand Lodge would designate one month as Scottish Rite Month for all of its lodges. The Scottish Rite Valleys would encourage every Scottish Rite Mason to attend the stated meeting of his own lodge for that month. Since rough statistics show that 30 percent of Scottish Rite Masons live away from their own home lodges, men would be encouraged to attend a local lodge as a guest.

During the first year, this would at least give many older lodge members a chance to mix with lodge brothers they had never met before. Extra effort should be put into encouraging attendance, perhaps even to the extent of telephoned invitations. At the meeting, the "long-lost" brothers should be brought up to date on lodge affairs and activities. Special events and efforts of the past ten years should be reviewed and discussed, and all current lodge officers introduced.

Undoubtedly, some of those Scottish Rite Masons will be able to talk about lodge events from earlier days, for there will be some present who have been members of that lodge for forty or fifty years. They can also talk about Scottish Rite: why they joined, what they feel they have gained, what the local Valley is doing. They can also answer practical questions that may well arise about what membership in Scottish Rite involves. (If Scottish Rite Valleys are seeking new members from the ranks of Master Masons, this is how it must be done, face-to-face.)

Both Scottish Rite and the Grand Lodge would have the same objective—new members—and there's nothing wrong with that. If each Scottish Rite Mason would be responsible for producing just *one* lodge petition *every five years*, Freemasonry would grow. The lodges would grow, and the appendant bodies would grow. (If you want the numbers, one million Scottish Rite Masons would then generate an average of two hundred thousand petitions per year.)

The same concept of a special lodge meeting would work with York Rite and the Shrine as well. They could be colorful meetings if the Knights Templar would wear their uniforms or mantles and the Shriners would wear their fezzes. Is *once a year* too much to ask?

I pose that question because I don't believe that lodges in general are given any real assistance when that assistance is largely limited to statements of support and encouragement from afar. I think that the real support will have to come from practical, working assistance and personal contact. Supporting appendant bodies must strive to give the lodges what they need. (That statement may prompt some to say, "Okay, wise guy, what *do* the lodges need?" And I will have to hang my head in embarrassment and answer, "I really don't know." I'm still searching for the answers, as are many grand officers and leaders of appendant bodies. All I can do here is to share what I have heard and observed.)

One point that must be made before discussing lodge meetings is that it is virtually impossible to generalize about any aspect of Masonic administration. There are fifty-one Grand Lodges with over thirteen thousand local lodges. It is entirely possible that every lodge problem I have heard about has been solved by one or more of those thousands of Masonic lodges. If so, I hope those successful lodges will speak up loud and clear, that all may learn.

By far the most common complaint I have heard, when trying to learn why lodge attendance is so low, is "Boring. Boring, boring, boring."

One point of view being espoused is that the fewer the meetings, the easier it is to assure that each one will be interesting. As mentioned earlier, one Grand Lodge is trying a program of just six lodge meetings a year. Others are considering a three- or four-month summer hiatus. (It should be remembered that in the earliest days of Masonry, the lodge met only for degree work or for very special purposes, so tradition dictates no set number of meetings in the year.)

A good speaker certainly makes a more interesting meeting, but most men I've talked to think that outside speakers are hard to get. They overlook all the groups in the local community who like the chance to tell their stories. Many of those groups have formal speakers' bureaus.

I believe that lodge members would enjoy listening to a representative from the local police department, sheriff's office, or state highway patrol (SWAT team speakers provide a fascinating evening). Speakers are usually available from the fire department or ambulance squad. A school principal might be invited to talk about problems with drugs and discipline. A minister or priest might discuss the basic beliefs of his faith and invite discussion. A group might be surprised at how interesting it can be to listen to someone from the fish and game service, the highway department, or even the sewer department. There's nothing wrong with a group of Masons learning more about the infrastructure of the community in which they live.

I was very impressed to see a directory of speakers published for its lodges by the Grand Lodge of Pennsylvania. That's a giant step in the right direction.

The only problem that presents itself in booking outside speakers is that they do not expect to talk to just seven or eight people. Twenty or thirty, or even more, are really required to justify a request for a speaker. One way to address that problem is to invite wives and older children. Non-Masonic friends could also be invited to attend.

If wives are invited, it is good to tie in dinner, but with a caution. Frequently (but not always), the lodge concept of "involving" their ladies is to have a dinner at which the wives prepare the food, set the tables, serve the food, clear the tables, and wash the dishes. That can't possibly meet anyone's definition of pleasurable involvement. I recall once asking my wife if she would like to go out to eat. When she replied in the affirmative, I asked where she would like to go. Her answer was educational. She said, "Any place where they do the cooking and wash the dishes!" The solution is to hire outside caterers.

The business portion of the meeting should be as brief as possible, to avoid keeping invited guests waiting too long. Their time could be occupied by a short talk, a brief Masonic video, or perhaps a drawing for door prizes.

As to the program itself, I am speaking as one who has appeared in many lodge rooms, both small and grand. Regardless of the room's size, the seating should be rearranged so that the speaker and audience can see each other easily. If the audience does not fill the available seats, ask them to close ranks and sit as closely together as possible, or to occupy the space along one wall, with the podium in front of them. (If you were reading your family a Christmas story, would you like them to move their chairs back against the four walls of the room?) The closer the speaker is to the people in the lodge room, the happier he or she will be with the arrangements.

For very large rooms, I would urge a portable public address system, so that speakers do not have to concern themselves with how loudly they must talk in order to be heard by everyone in the room, or how long they can last before getting hoarse. My suggestion, of course, is that every room be made speaker-friendly. Word does get around about such things.

Another approach to achieving interesting meetings is being tried in some areas. It is the "Masonic forum," or "town meeting," approach. It is good because the lodge members are involved, not just entertained. It consists of a ten-minute talk on a Masonic topic, followed by a round-table discussion. It is much more effective if chaired by a caring man who makes an effort to get everyone present to express an opinion. There are always those in any group who need no coaxing to volunteer their opinions about everything. The trick is to extract an opinion or comment from those members who usually don't speak up. Regardless of how quiet they may be, they will often surprise their brothers by offering a balanced, objective opinion, or some valuable insight into the topic under consideration. And they in turn are usually pleased that their views are sought and appreciated. (Even a misunderstanding is food for thought . . . and discussion.)

An open forum meeting with women included may be a revelation to all, if the ladies can be persuaded to open up. Many of them hold strong opinions—I have been surprised by some that have been expressed to me—and they would probably feel good about having an opportunity to air matters that particularly interest and concern them.

Increased attendance is worthy of extra effort. Try calling attention to what promises to be a special meeting. Conduct a phone campaign and extend personal invitations. Tell absentee members that they are missed, that their brothers have heard about them and want to meet them. And above all, make every man feel welcome!

Set goals for the year. Freemasonry will grow rapidly and keep growing if each lodge will produce just six petitions each year for each one hundred lodge members. That's almost impossible to achieve year after year, of course, if the entire burden falls on the eight or nine of those hundred men who regularly attend meetings. The non-attenders have got to be involved as well, if only by phone or letter.

Make a survey of all lodge members to identify the names and ages of all male children or grandchildren. That's the membership gold mine, if watched and worked. Send birthday cards. Plan events for boys, or events for the whole family.

Masonic friendship events deserve very special consideration in planning and presentation to prevent them from degenerating into tedious discourses. Videos can often help. There are many good ones available now; just ask around. One of the best short ones I've seen—about fifteen minutes—was produced by the Grand Lodge of Massachusetts. The best feature-length video, lasting about one hour, is *Unseen Journey*, produced by the Grand Lodge of Illinois. It's long enough to include a symphony orchestra, costume drama, film clips of Sean Connery and Michael Caine from *The Man Who Would Be King*, and photographs of the lodge in Bannack, Montana, whose members turned into vigilantes to drive the outlaws and murderers out of nearby gold camps. Another is *On the Wings of Words*, hosted by Ernest Borgnine, produced by the Southern Jurisdiction of Scottish Rite.

The plain truth is that it is difficult to help lodges unless they identify and admit the help they need. Think about it, talk, analyze, offer suggestions, be specific. Share your feelings (and your successes!) with your district officers and your Grand Lodge.

There is a great deal being said these days about helping the symbolic lodges with attendance and new members. Several programs have been launched. Clearly, however, there is no faster or more effective help to the local lodge than that provided by the lodge itself. Besides, the help you give yourself is the most reliable, and by far the most rewarding.

16

"God Loveth a Cheerful Giver"

ONE AFTERNOON I was on a program out of San Antonio,
Texas. The usual calls were coming in, for and against
Freemasonry. After a couple of negative calls, a woman
got on the air and opened with: "You just can't imagine the anger that
is growing in me at those nasty things being said against the Masons!"
Then she told her own story.

As a little girl in Idaho during World War II, she was always
weak and in pain. Finally, her condition was diagnosed as a rare heart
problem. She needed surgery to save her life, but with most surgeons
away on active duty, the only two hospitals her doctor could locate
that were qualified to undertake that surgery were in Southern
California and in Ann Arbor, Michigan.

The Michigan hospital agreed to take her, but advised her
doctor that because of military needs they had no backup blood
supply. The girl's family would have to arrange privately for eighteen
pints of blood of her type. Local inquiries to hospitals and blood
banks produced no results and her parents were despondent.

When her grandfather joined the family for Sunday dinner, he
noticed the subdued atmosphere and after dinner asked the reason
for all the gloom in the house. The parents told him of the problem

with the blood supply, and she said, "My grandfather hugged me and said, 'Don't you worry, sweetheart, I'll take care of it!'" Her father, she continued, was very upset and loudly expressed his anger with her grandfather. He reprimanded him for making a promise to a sick child that he knew he couldn't keep. Her grandfather didn't even reply, but put on his coat and left the house.

A couple of weeks later her grandfather came to her home again, this time with the news that he had the blood all lined up, "and a couple of pints to spare." Her father was stunned, and asked his father how he had managed to do what the hospitals couldn't do. He answered that he had contacted his Masonic lodge brothers. Some of them had volunteered to call me they knew in other lodges and at the Grand Lodge. The pledges were made and kept and the little girl went to Ann Arbor for successful surgery. Before long, she could run and play with her friends. She ended her call with: "That was almost fifty years ago, and every night since then I have thanked God in my prayers for the Freemasons. If those men hadn't cared so much about a child they had never met, I wouldn't be here today."

Who could express the spirit of Masonic giving better than that? The whole atmosphere of the show changed, and so did the ensuing calls. There is little doubt that the general public will react very favorably to Masonic giving, but unfortunately they hear very little about it.

First, there is the concept instilled into many of us as children that good deeds should be done quietly and in private. Somehow they lost their value if they were discovered or – worse still – became the subject of bragging. Today that attitude has changed considerably, as welfare agencies, health-care groups, and even religious bodies have established extensive public relations departments. They want the world to know the good they are doing, because that publicity helps to boost memberships and contributions. Perhaps it is time that the Masons joined in with the mainstream thinking of contemporary caregiving. They have a lot to report.

Recently the Grand Secretary of the Masons of Pennsylvania decided to relax for a couple of hours on a Saturday afternoon by listening to the Penn State football game. His weekend relaxation was interrupted by a long-distance call from Texas. The caller explained that she was with the Women's Aid Society. A young woman had approached them for assistance in getting to her sister in a small town in New Jersey. Her sister had been injured and had to be brought home to Texas. The only thing she knew about the town's location was that Philadelphia was the nearest municipal airport. Women's Aid had put the woman on a plane that would land in Philadelphia in about an hour, but when she arrived she would be totally lost.

The Women's Aid counselor was eager to help the distraught young woman but had very little to go on. She was grasping at a straw that had surfaced during their interview, when the young woman had mentioned that her "daddy had been a Mason." The counselor had called the Grand Lodge of Texas, where someone had given her the phone number of the Grand Lodge of Pennsylvania. Fortunately, one of the staff who had come in to do some Saturday catch-up work took the call and gave her the home phone number of the Grand Secretary of Pennsylvania. Could he please help the Mason's daughter?

The Grand Secretary, whose home was in Philadelphia, did not delegate the assignment or try to find some other Mason to handle it. He drove to the Philadelphia airport himself and spent hours trying to locate the young stranger from Texas. From a brother Mason in the airport security department he learned the location of the New Jersey town where the injured sister lived. With almost no public transportation available, he decided to drive her there himself. On the way, the Texas visitor told him that she needed to rent a truck so that she could transport her sister home to Texas with her furniture and clothing. She was hoping to leave the next day.

Arriving at the home of the injured sister, the Grand Secretary cast around for others to help out. He had the good fortune to find his Delaware counterpart at home. After explaining the dilemma, he was promptly assured that four Masons would arrive the next morning to help the ladies rent a truck and load up for their trip to Texas.

That taken care of, the Grand Secretary scrounged for empty corrugated cartons at local stores. Then he helped the women to pack their linens, kitchenware, china, and clothing. By the time the job was finished it was three o'clock in the morning, and he took off for his home in Philadelphia, tired but happy.

As promised, four Masons from a lodge in Delaware showed up at the door the next morning. They arranged for a truck rental, then loaded the boxes and the furniture. When the task was completed they stood by the road, smiling and waving good-bye to the two young women who had had their prayers answered and were now safely headed for Texas.

Three Masonic Grand Lodges across the country had been involved; five individual Masons had not hesitated to forego their planned weekend activities in order to provide speedy help in the emergency. They gave of their time and their money in a spirit of cheerful goodwill. The beneficiaries of that kindness were two daughters of a Texas Mason, whom they had never seen before and would in all likelihood never see again. Their compassion could not have been extended in hope of enjoying any kind of reward. There may be someone who will read this story with a puzzled frown and wonder why those men acted as they did. I can guarantee that that puzzled person will never understand Freemasonry.

There might be someone who saw those four men loading a truck with furniture and boxes on a Sunday morning and criticized them for not being at church. As far as I'm concerned, they were indeed engaged in religious worship. ("Inasmuch as ye have done it unto one of the least of these my brethren, ye have done it unto me.")

Such tales of individual Masonic charity abound.

Sometimes the entire lodge participates—for example, to help the widow and children of a departed brother, or to conduct a Christmas fund drive. One lodge noticed the rather bare grounds of a nearby home for the elderly and spent a weekend planting trees for their future enjoyment. A lodge in California bought building materials, provided their own tools, and spent their spare time repairing, painting, and installing safety features in the home of an elderly couple struggling to get by on a very limited income. Another lodge provided the food, the games, and the prizes for a picnic held for a local school for the blind.

Operating on a statewide basis, the fifty-one Grand Lodges, of course, have much larger memberships and far greater resources than the individual lodges. More than two-thirds of the Grand Lodges maintain Masonic homes for elderly Masons and their wives or widows, while a number of them have children's homes for orphaned and abandoned youngsters, who need have no Masonic connection. Drug- and alcohol-abuse programs also receive widespread Grand Lodge support. Many Grand Lodges run special charitable programs of their own, such as support for the Special Olympics, highway litter patrol, and free Christmas and Thanksgiving dinners for the needy.

All of the appendant Masonic systems sponsor meaningful charitable efforts, often helping those who would otherwise have nowhere to turn. The York Rite Knights Templar support the Templar Eye Foundation, which takes care of vision problems for young and old, especially for those with limited income and no applicable insurance coverage. Children receive corrective eye surgery not only to improve vision, but also to correct defects such as cross-eye that all too often make children the tearful butt of cruel remarks from unthinking classmates. The elderly benefit from free cataract surgery and treatment from degenerative eye diseases that could cause blindness if left untreated. All are eligible for help if eyeglasses or contact lenses are needed.

The smaller appendant Masonic systems have found their own worthwhile projects through which to help the less fortunate. The Grottoes of North America fill an important need with their program to provide dentistry for handicapped children, whose dental problems are often beyond the scope of the family dentist. The first problem presents itself when the dentist says, "Open wide." The normal child responds instantly: The handicapped child may be quite unable to do so, for a variety of reasons. Sometimes the structure of the child's jaw may be distorted. Effective treatment for the disabled requires special training and—often—special equipment. Those services are available through Grotto support in Illinois, Ohio, and many other jurisdictions.

The most significant charity of the Tall Cedars of Lebanon rises from the members' dedication to the unique problems of children suffering from muscular dystrophy. In the last decade they have contributed over half a million dollars to the National Muscular Dystrophy Telethon. They fund supportive grants to physicians working in the field and have instituted a program of related scholarships. Their concern is evidenced by far more personal acts than simple check writing. Through a program of hospital visitations, Christmas and holiday parties, and individual attention, they reach out to brighten the lives of children trapped in their mysterious physical prisons.

Scottish Rite Masonry has been embraced by about one million Master Masons in the United States. The system is divided into two jurisdictions, each headed by a Supreme Council of 33rd degree Masons. The Northern Jurisdiction, based in Lexington, Massachusetts, covers fifteen northeastern states and has about four hundred thousand members. The Southern Jurisdiction, headquartered in Washington, D.C., covers the other thirty-five states, with over half a million members.

Outstanding among the many good works carried out within the Southern Jurisdiction Scottish Rite are two beautiful and superbly equipped hospitals for children: The Texas Scottish Rite Hospital for Children at Dallas, and the Scottish Rite Children's Medical Center at Atlanta. The latter is an awesome facility that is said to have provided the inspiration for the Shrine hospitals program. Scottish Rite Valleys in Alabama and Tennessee fund programs to ensure that every needy schoolchild has new shoes and socks to wear. The Valley of Knoxville alone has given out approximately one hundred and forty thousand pairs of new shoes.

Almost everyone knows of a child who just cannot master reading and writing skills. They are frequently regarded by their teachers, and even their parents, as retarded, or "slow learners." Even worse is life for the child who cannot master simple speech, often to the point of not being able to express a single coherent sentence. Children shackled by that handicap often suffer from mounting frustration because they cannot make their thoughts and needs understood. That frustration can build into violent explosions of anger that involve hurling anything they can lift, and striking anyone within reach. The outbursts are accompanied by crying and screaming, causing violent disruptions to all around them. Historically, such children have been branded "emotionally disturbed," or as victims of mental illness.

About twenty years ago some Scottish Rite Masons in Colorado hit upon the inspired concept of establishing and funding a clinic to help these victims of learning disorders. The clinic filled a desperate need, and the idea was embraced by Southern Jurisdiction Scottish Rite Masons across the country. Now there are about a hundred of them, from coast to coast and from the Mexican border to the Canadian. There is even one in Alaska.

Some clinics are staffed and operated by the local Scottish Rite Valley, while others operate within local children's medical centers, with the Scottish Rite Masons providing the funding. Each clinic operates with trained specialists, including professional pathologists and therapists. The treatment rooms are equipped with one-way mirrors, so that parents can watch and learn how to continue the therapy at home. Scottish Rite Masons, their wives, and their older children volunteer to provide transportation, do clerical work, or take care of any other tasks that may be needed.

Not surprisingly, Northern Jurisdiction Masons have watched the operation and growth of the centers and are impressed. Some of them have decided to establish Childood Language Disorders Centers in their own areas, with the full blessings of the Southern Jurisdiction, so we may soon see these centers for aphasia and dyslexia in every state of the union.

For almost sixty years, the major charitable effort of the Northern Jurisdiction has been to promote research into the causes and treatment of schizophrenia. This destructive psychosis is the most prevalent and debilitating of all mental illnesses. The ongoing support has involved channeling many millions of dollars into research fellowships and recurring grants to researchers associated with major universities and medical centers.

Best known by far of all the Masonic-related charities are the Shrine hospitals: nineteen hospitals for crippled children and three Shrine Burns Institutes for badly burned children. The most extraordinary aspect of those hospitals, especially in today's world of shattering medical costs, is that they have no billing departments. The expert medical and nursing care is provided entirely free of charge. No attempts are made to collect from medical insurance plans, and there are no government subsidies. The cost of maintaining the hospitals is covered by the Shriners' fund-raising projects, by an assessment on annual dues, and through successful efforts to build an impressive endowment fund.

The nineteen orthopedic hospitals for crippled children are located from coast to coast, as well as in Honolulu, Mexico City, and Montreal. These hospitals specialize in the treatment of children suffering from birth defects and deformities, as well as those handicapped by diseases or injuries affecting the spine, bones, and joints. Artificial limbs, wheelchairs, and other necessary equipment are provided as required, also free of charge.

The three Shrine Burns Institutes are located at Boston, Galveston, and Cincinnati. Many regard them as the preeminent world centers for the treatment of severely burned children, and small patients are brought to the centers regardless of the distance involved.

Most burned children are delivered to the Shrine Burns Institutes as soon as possible after their accidents; but many patients are victims who have already received treatment elsewhere. Although declared "cured," they are frequently left unable to use limbs and are therefore in need of corrective surgery. Others may have been left horribly disfigured; they come to the Shrine unit for restorative and plastic surgery.

At the Burns Institutes, a program of research has led to increasingly effective forms of treatment, and lives are now being saved that would have been lost just a few years ago.

The free services extend well beyond the hands-on medical care to such considerations as transportation to and from the hospitals for both patients and parents. If they cannot afford hotel accommodations on their own, living accommodations near the hospital are provided for parents for the duration of the treatment. Braces, wheelchairs, and artificial limbs are also provided where needed, as is training in their use. Nor are physical and psychological therapy overlooked.

Over three hundred thousand children of all nationalities, races, and religions have benefited from this extraordinary program, nor does any injured child need any Masonic connection to qualify for treatment. Countless more will benefit from the intense ongoing research programs at each center, which have already achieved impressive improvements in methods of diagnosis and treatment.

I expect that any Freemason I meet could add a list of Masonic charities that have not been mentioned here. I could do that myself, but the examples given should be sufficient to demonstrate that every community benefits from the presence of Freemasonry in its midst.

Some may wonder how much these extensive Masonic charities cost. The answer is about $1.5 million *per day*, or well over $500 million each year.

One would imagine that these outstanding, humane programs would be universally admired, but, unfortunately, certain anti-Masonic bigots disapprove. Some fundamentalists charge that these charitable works are so prolific that Masonry must teach a religious doctrine of salvation through good works. Such an accusation contradicts the most basic tenet of Freemasonry, which says that each Mason must find the pathway to salvation through his own religious faith. Anyone who tries to twist the spirit of selfless giving that motivates, energizes, and nourishes these charitable institutions by alleging a plot to preach a false religion is either willfully ignorant, morbidly envious, or perhaps some of each.

Every Mason, be he Christian, Jew, or Muslim, fully believes that in helping those less fortunate than himself he is living God's word.

And just one small point to wrap up this discussion: A young man planning to become a Mason may read all this and think that he is about to join a fraternity that will constantly beat on him for charitable contributions. That's simply not true. Every Mason is told repeatedly that he is not to support any Masonic endeavor to the point that it will jeopardize the life-style of his own family, or affect his contributions to his own church.

Every Mason's help is appreciated, but only to the extent that it is freely given from funds that are available for that purpose, and with the full knowledge and support of his wife. When a man casts his bread upon the waters, it usually comes from his purse. When it returns many-fold, it is firmly lodged in his heart. And don't let *anyone* tell you that God is not pleased.

17

"Let Your Light So Shine . . ."

I N THE EARLY days of my business career I held positions in both sales management and public relations. The objectives of a sales department are very easy to define. They are to get purchase orders. The goals of a public relations department are much more elusive. They relate to sales, of course, but reach beyond that to bear on every facet of corporate operations, including top management. My experience led me to identify the goal of the PR department as building an "atmosphere of acceptance" for the company: for its products, its services, its employment practices, and its treatment of shareholders. In other words, to create an image of being "good guys."

Freemasonry is in urgent need of an "atmosphere of acceptance" with the general public, a totally justifiable image of God-fearing, dedicated, generous, and compassionate men with a high regard for family values, for their roles in their churches, and for the plights of the less fortunate. The high regard of the general public would provide the incentive for men to join the ranks of Freemasonry and would act as a shield against the fanatical attacks of men who have discovered the pathway to power by finding Satan under every rock.

Organizations, like individuals, have both a *reputation*, which is what you are thought to be, and a *character*, which is what you really are. If your reputation is better than your character, you will be found out sooner or later; so you shouldn't spend time and money trying to convince people that you are good men. On the other hand, if, as I think is true of Freemasonry, your true character is much better than your reputation, you have a golden opportunity.

Consider what the public hears today. When a Southern Baptist pastor in Tennessee was arrested for sexual abusing young boys in his congregation, and a Catholic priest in Ohio was convicted on similar charges, the press was sympathetic toward the church leaders who had to bear this terrible burden. When a Demolay advisor in Kansas was arrested on the very same allegations, the Order of Demolay was instantly condemned as a "cult" by local media.

During the past year there was a full-page article about Freemasonry in the *Washington Times* (part of Reverend Moon's media empire). It dwelt at length on the strange, seemingly demonic symbols of the Craft. The writer did admit that many important figures throughout American history, and in American industry, had been Freemasons, but said that they are all dead now. He told his readers that *today* no important people are Masons. Of course, it would do no good to provide that reporter with a list of important American Freemasons who are very much alive today. Even if he recognizes his error, he will shrug it off. He is not going to correct the false information that he published for tens of thousands of readers, so his opinions will stand as truth. No one will take him to task for his deliberate distortions.

The same thing is true of the anti-Masonic evangelists. It serves no purpose to make direct appeals to Pat Robertson, James L. Holly, or John Ankerberg. It is a waste of time trying to find an opening into closed minds. They are broadcasting their Masonic condemnations to a wide public audience, and it is to that broad audience that Freemasonry must take its message.

When Masonry leaves a great void in the world of public information, it cannot surprise anyone that negative publicity is believed. If a man standing in a crowded room is approached by an angry accuser who brands him a disgusting criminal, and he stands there with his jaw clamped shut and his lips pressed together, offering not a single word in his own defense, no one can blame the onlookers for concluding that since the man didn't defend himself, he must be guilty.

We can hardly blame others for that reaction. What are our own feelings when we read of a man or an organization accused of wrongdoing, then read that the accused "could not be reached for comment," "refused to take our calls," or simply responded, "No comment"? Doesn't that refusal to respond arouse our suspicions? So why do Masons remain tight-lipped in the face of scurrilous attacks on the fraternity?

While many regard that stoic silence as an inviolable Masonic tradition, I see it as a great disservice to Masons and their families, and one of the greatest deterrents to recruitment. One must bear in mind that there is no Masonic tradition that speaks against a Masonic body asserting itself, what it does, what it believes, what it stands for.

The one Masonic body that has learned that lesson is the Shrine, which also has the tremendous advantage of a national office and a central hierarchy that can easily speak with one voice. It has done so on occasion, and it hasn't hesitated to speak up to defend itself when attacked, as it did in the allegations of the misuse of hospital funds. Most important, that defense was successful. Perhaps that's the reason that the fundamentalist attacks on Masonry tend more and more to avoid accusations against the Shrine and its charities.

The Shrine is the only Masonic system with a director of public relations and a PR department. They have made the Shrine hospital program known across the country, and I have never heard one word of criticism of the PR function in that Masonic body.

When suggestions have been made in favor of a national Masonic PR program, the standard objection has been that such a program is virtually impossible because of the structure of fifty-one separate Grand Lodge jurisdictions. I'll admit that the system may make the concept of a central Masonic voice more difficult, but it does not by any means render the task impossible. There are hundreds of examples in this country of separate companies with separate ownership, separate management, and variations in product lines, who nevertheless join together in trade associations. Their principal purpose is PR programs that represent all the entities, but don't compete with the PR programs of the individual members. Companies join trade associations because they recognize that there are occasions when a combined voice speaks with more power than that of any one associate.

Another argument in favor of a central voice is that the major media usually speak to a national audience and are therefore most attracted to issues and events that will be of interest to the entire sweep of their readers, listeners, or viewers, rather than those of primarily local interest.

One day during the past year I traveled to Massachusetts to be interviewed about Masonry for a full hour on a radio program beamed to sixty-two cities. That afternoon I drove into Boston for a fifteen-minute Masonic interview on a national cable TV network show. If I can accept the audience figures provided by the two networks, about four and a half million people heard some positive observations about Masonry on that one day. That kind of impact needs to be repeated many times over.

The most immediate benefit is the reaction of Masons and their families. They appreciate hearing good things about the fraternity. It makes them proud and helps to overcome the incipient frustration and depression caused by all the fundamentalist Mason-bashing, which is generally all that radio listeners and TV viewers experience in the way of Masonic comment and appraisal.

One important point in favor of a national Masonic PR program is the incredible rate at which network radio and TV gobble up material. They are constantly hungry for more news, more information, more entertainment; anything that will help to fill those thousands of hours of broadcast time every week. Programming ideas that are well thought-out and professionally presented should find ready acceptance.

Nor will those ideas be limited to responses to Masonic critics. Answering anti-Masons, especially in circumstances such as the present Southern Baptist Convention crisis, will always be part of any well-managed public relations program, but by no means would it be the entire effort. As important as crisis management may be, it is not more important than a well thought-out, long-range agenda.

Masonic activities have much to contribute to what promises to be a long-range concern for social issues. Health care is one area. Care for children, both physical and mental, is a primary concern. So are the threats to individual freedoms that appear to be growing. Freemasonry could provide rich material to reports on all of those issues, including data, anecdotes and photo opportunities. The important point is that the agencies putting such TV programs or written stories together must be made aware of the information and support that Masonry can give them. (Such enhanced media awareness of Masonry is a job best done by PR professionals.)

Special events provide opportunities for Masonic PR. It was a great pleasure to see the reenactment of the Masonic laying of the White House cornerstone on CNN. Another might be a ceremonious delivery of the Masonic Bible so often used for the inauguration of U.S. presidents since it was used first at the swearing-in of George Washington. There are such events all the time, and they must be dramatized and made known to national media.

That doesn't mean that local and regional media should be ignored. If there is an exciting story to be told about the involvement of Freemasons in Texas (and there is), it will obviously be more interesting to Texans than to anyone else. The growing popularity of radio call-in shows is a gold mine of opportunity for local and regional programs. If there are half a dozen radio talk shows in a given market, each of which would like to have a different guest every day, five days a week, that means opportunities for over fifteen hundred guests a year in that one market.

A convenient factor is that most call-in shows can be participated in by phone from home or office. It's not as human as being in the studio with the host, but it works. The participation is usually planned no more than two or three weeks in advance. Sometimes guest appearances can be arranged by a direct call to the station, or one can purchase an ad in a directory of available guests which is used by show hosts and producers to line up programming.

Obviously, any local Masonic body can use this form of public education. All that's required is a good explanation of what the Masonic guest is prepared to talk about, such as a local charitable event or an ongoing program, like the local Children's Language Disorders Center. The speaker selected should have a thorough knowledge of his subject and be ready to answer questions as they come in.

The matter of selecting a spokesman is difficult, and sometimes delicate. There are plenty of good men who talk too fast, or don't speak clearly, or are given to atrocious grammar. They may be good men, but they don't make good spokesmen on radio or TV.

Much more difficult to appraise is a man's ability to think on his feet, to answer clearly (and correctly), and to *stay calm*, however great the provocation. (There will be those who will now remind me of times I lost my temper with some bombastic bigot on radio call-in shows. I can only plead guilty.)

The delicate part enters in when someone clearly unsuitable as a question-answering spokesman volunteers for the job, convinced of his own communication skills. Political parties have to deal with that problem all the time. It calls for great tact, well laced with consideration for the good attitude of the man who wants to help.

A radio-show guest should bear in mind that talk shows thrive on controversy. The producer usually judges the success of the program by the number of phone calls that come in. The host may stir up a little controversy himself, and thereby rattle the Masonic guest. One host told me, "Look, I'm sympathetic to the Masons. My father is a 32nd, and loves it. But don't be surprised if I play devil's advocate and ask questions that may annoy you. I want to stimulate my listeners to get into the act."

By far the majority of radio talk-show hosts are polite and considerate and try to make their guests comfortable. Notable exceptions are the so-called "Christian" stations. For them, the purpose of inviting a speaker to talk favorably about Freemasonry is usually to make the guest the embarrassed target of public accusations of Satan worship and acts against God. They welcome callers who ask questions, or make comments, in the same anti-Masonic vein.

I had a call from a radio producer in North Carolina inviting me to take part in a one-hour program about Freemasonry, and I accepted. On the scheduled day I was called and told to stand by for two minutes as the show was introduced. Then I heard an announcer saying, "Welcome to your Christian Radio Forum. Today, our topic will be the Freemasons, the last in our series on the Strange Cults of the World." For the next hour I was called a "friend of the devil-cult," a "Unitarian in spirit," and a "personal agent of Satan" for speaking favorably of Freemasonry. I would agree with anyone who stated that such a show has no place in a Masonic PR program, although such programming is becoming more and more common.

One day I was called with, "We understand that you are available to talk about Masons. Do you have evidence that they worship Satan or any of his demons?" When I replied that I didn't believe that such evidence existed, the caller said, "Too bad. That would have made an interesting program." I'm not certain which one of us hung up first.

If it is determined that a national Masonic public relations office should be set up, the first priority would be to make its existence known to the media. Historically, the press is accustomed to the idea that it's almost impossible to find a Masonic spokesman to address any issue, so they must be told that things have changed.

To be most effective a PR department would need not just financial support, but a constant supply of newsworthy information from all Masonic bodies. Grand Lodges, in particular, would need to supply news of their activities that are worthy of public attention. The wonderful work, for example, of resident Masons and their wives in Saudi Arabia during the Gulf War, when they spared no effort to be of service to the American forces, was a story worth telling, but it was never told. And all significant anecdotes related to major charitable activities should be sent to the public relations office.

A central public relations office could also produce PR manuals to help local and regional Masonic bodies get publicity in their own areas, with tips on the types of stories and photographs most likely to end up in print, or on broadcast media.

The logistics of setting up an effective PR program would have to be carefully addressed. The simplest method would appear to be to expand the Masonic Service Association, already the arm of the Grand Lodges. In addition to its work in disseminating information to Masons, it could have a department—perhaps called the Masonic Public Information Service—to disseminate information to the general public.

Such a program, run by dedicated, experienced professionals and supported with a flow of information from Masonic bodies, would inject a constant stream of positive impressions about Freemasonry into the public consciousness. The long-term benefits of those positive views should not be difficult to imagine. What is there that would not be easier, more satisfying, or more rewarding about Masonic endeavors if much of the world would hold Masonry in high regard? And even more important, an enlightened public could effectively disarm the anti-Masonic zealots.

I realize that there will be Masons who will object to the very thought of Masons "striking back," and some Christian Masons may feel that the Craft should continue to heed Jesus' admonition to turn the other cheek. For them, I would offer another admonition by Jesus from the same sermon, when he said (Matthew 5:16), "Let your light so shine before men, that they may see your good works, and glorify your Father which is in heaven."

So mote it be.

18

Decision

THIS WILL BE the last book I write as a non-Mason.

I have decided to become a Freemason, which is why I dedicated this book to all those who will make that same decision.

Certainly no one can say that this is a decision into which I dashed blindly, without thinking it through. I spent years delving into the origins and history of the Craft, from the Middle Ages through the founding of our country, and more years mixing with Freemasons in every aspect of the Masonic structure. I have had long conversations with those who love it and with those who would like to see Masonry totally wiped out. I have carefully weighed the arguments for and against Freemasonry and have spent many hours tracking down quotations and scriptural references presented as "evidence" by rabid anti-Masons.

I took their accusations seriously, having no reason not to. As a non-Mason I was not committed emotionally to any position. On the other hand, I had some knowledge of the historical arguments, mandated by prejudice rather than logic, by which religious groups attack others. I know that some religions are structured to promulgate hatred and bigotry, but I will never believe that Christianity is one of them.

It is understandable that when a man has decided on the religion that merits his total belief and allegiance, he will stand convinced that his religion alone is *right*. So it follows that he will believe that all other religions are in error to varying degrees—the degree determined by how far their beliefs diverge from *his* own understanding of God's truth. On that basis, he can thunder and storm against every other man's faith, convinced that in so doing he is following God's will. He thinks that this reaction is righteous indignation, but I think that it is better defined as *self*-righteous indignation.

In a nation—and indeed a world—such as ours, there are peoples of widely diverse religions, and there always will be. The big question, then, is whether it is more constructive to constantly berate, harangue, and condemn all those whose beliefs are held to be in error, in the expectation of pleasing God, or rather to find ways for all men to live together, promoting one's own religious beliefs only with love and by example, instead of through militant aggression.

Freemasons obviously feel that it *is* possible for all men who subscribe to a moral religious faith to meet and act together for the good of all. I favor their approach. I have studied too many centuries of destructive wars, religious persecution, and physical torture to feel otherwise.

Many anti-Masons condemn Masonry because they say that it recognizes all religions as equal, and so the one true religion—their own—is denigrated by being classified as being no better or worse than any other, instead of being properly acknowledged as the one supreme revelation of God's will. This was one of the chief complaints Pope Leo XIII had against Freemasonry in his famous condemnation in 1884. That misunderstanding still stands as a barrier between Masonry and official Catholic church doctrine, over one hundred years later.

The simple truth is that Masonry does *not* recognize all religions as equal. To do so would require making a careful investigation, evaluation, and judgment of all faiths, which Masons have never done. Instead, Masonry recognizes the equal *right* of all men to worship God as they see fit. Religious zealots abhor the concept of the free and equal right to worship according to one's conscience. They instead often eliminate it by law, if they succeed in getting political control in areas where there are no constitutional safeguards for individual rights. We have seen it happen in Franco's Spain, in Iran under Khomeini, and even today in the Sudan. (And those who say that no one wants such a thing to happen *here* should read some of the fundamentalist works I've been studying.)

Perhaps some of them do not see their drive for religious supremacy as a movement to control the political rights and personal lives of others, but the power-driven leaders among them certainly do. And if, as they apparently believe, Freemasonry is a major barrier to their ambitions, I want to be a part of that barrier.

Masons are condemned because they are against intolerance, imposture, superstition, and fanaticism, each of which words the Southern Baptist evangelist Dr. James L. Holly says "is a synonym of revealed, God-centered religion." It seems that his God hates religious tolerance. He defines "superstition" as the true Christian faith, and "fanaticism" as the only proper mode of conduct for a Christian. Dr. Holly certainly tries his best to live up to his own conclusions, but I simply do not agree with him. The first Bible verse I ever learned, in a Sunday school kindergarten, was "God is Love." Whatever happened to that concept? Nothing, as far as I am concerned. It is as true for me today as it was then.

I have now mixed with Masons who are at the top of giant corporations and Masons who hold down factory jobs. I have talked to Christian Masons, Jewish Masons, and Muslim Masons. None of them perceives any conflict between the teachings of his faith and the Masonic principles he experiences in the lodge.

I do not write about Masonic charities which I have only read about. I have visited Scottish Rite Language Disorders Centers for children held back in life by problems with written or spoken language. I have visited Masonic "shoe stores" with full inventories and customer conveniences. The only thing missing was a cash register, for these shops distribute free shoes to needy schoolchildren. I've listened to expressions of gratitude from bright young people who have received Masonic scholarships for higher education. I've talked to elderly people whose sight had been saved by surgery they could not have afforded on their own, surgery that was paid for by the Masonic Knights Templar.

I've watched Masons pay thousands of entry fees for children in the Special Olympics, with the beautiful explanation that parents of a handicapped child already have too many financial burdens.

It was more than just informative to visit a Shrine Burns Institute; it was traumatic. The start of my visit was peaceful: an impressive building, a beautiful lobby and waiting area. I sat with my hosts in a paneled conference room and discussed the treatment from diagnosis through medication and therapy. We talked about prosthetic devices for the patients who had lost limbs, or the use of them. I learned about plastic surgery and the efforts to overcome disfigurement to the greatest possible extent, to help the child grow up to assume as near normal a role in society as possible. We talked about the outpatient services that provide continuing care, often for years. We discussed the burns treatment research program, which may be the best in the world. We even talked about the transportation and accommodation for parents, some of whom travel to the centers from outside the country.

And it's all free! Is there another hospital system in America with no billing department? All very gratifying and praiseworthy. All impressive—but none of it helps to prepare one for being with the children themselves.

Most of them were hurt because of accidents. They don't, and can't, understand what has happened to them. The agony of burns is without equal, and these children are the most severe cases. They are often mutilated and monstrously disfigured, sometimes suffering the loss of ears, noses, and lips. The indescribable scarring is the challenge facing the surgeons who carry out restorative and reconstructive procedures.

The children show remarkable courage and resilience in heartbreaking circumstances. In their presence, the only bright eyes in the room are theirs. My stomach writhed and tangled in knots. I stand in awe of the Shrine volunteers who get the children to the hospitals and give their services there. I know that I would be of no help to them: I would spend most of the time mopping my eyes.

To support these twenty-two free hospitals the Shriners pay out over a *million dollars a day*, and it's worth every penny of it. Such great expenditures and widespread operations require careful budgeting and cost controls, but I learned one day that the budgets are only guides; they do not determine or limit the care.

I was sitting in an informal session with some of the Shriners who were directors of the Shrine Burns Institute in Cincinnati. They were discussing a very difficult and unexpected case of severe burns that was to arrive at the hospital the following day. The complexity and anticipated length of the treatments needed was a subject of concern to the directors. Finally, one man said, "I guess it comes down to whether it will fit into our budget." Another Shriner responded, "No, what it comes down to is that whatever this little girl needs, that's our budget." They all agreed.

That's what Masonry really is. It's the men in it. And they are the primary reason for my decision. No one has to tell me that these men believe that God is Love. I have seen that for myself, over and over again.

Those who know me have learned that I am fascinated by the rich tapestry of medieval history. Probing the origins of Free-masonry was a totally absorbing project for me, but I do not insist that others agree with my findings. Origins can be important, but they are not paramount. Nor are the ceremonies, titles, and symbols the reasons for my decision. They could be other ceremonies, other titles, and other symbols, and I would still have the same interest in becoming a Freemason. I will support those that exist because of a deep feeling for tradition, but to me they are not the heart of Masonry.

The heart of Masonry is in the hearts of its members. There was a time in my life when I would have considered that there was nothing extraordinary about a dedication to moral conduct, individual free-doms, charitable good works, and a meeting of men of all creeds in brotherhood. I thought that those were values and beliefs held by everyone. Now I have learned that this is not so. There was a time in my innocent, younger days when I imagined that just being an American was to be a member of a select brotherhood. Now, I see some men wrap the flag around themselves, declare that they are superpatriots, and preach doctrines that are in effect clarion calls to tear up the Bill of Rights.

Do I find myself caught in a dilemma, trying to choose between Christian bigotry and Christian bounty? I don't. Nor, I think, will my decision meet with the disapproval of Him who told the parable of the Good Samaritan and preached the Sermon on the Mount.

Strangely enough, Masonry may be the only organization on the face of the earth that practices, to its detriment, the scriptural admonition to turn the other cheek. Masons have suffered generations of abuse stemming from false allegations and rarely have answered back.

Masons all over the country have shared with me their feelings that it is time for change, time for Freemasonry to speak out, and I fully agree. But if I am going to exhort Masons to stand up for what they believe, it seems only proper that I follow my own advice and take the ultimate stand to verify the sincerity of my beliefs.

I have delayed the decision for a long time, since I discovered that many radio and television stations, even networks, would welcome a guest who could speak about Freemasonry objectively, a guest not himself a Mason. I have been doing that for the past two years.

At the same time, I have carried out a busy schedule, speaking to Masonic bodies, and have met more good men and made more new friends in those two years than in the prior twenty. I have a duty to them, too.

During a break at a Masonic conference in Indianapolis, I sat over a cup of coffee with a Christian minister who is also a 33rd degree Mason. I was expressing my growing guilt for all the time I was spending away from my wife, because of Masonic travel. I cited months when I have not been with her for a single weekend. He said, "There's an easy way to stop all that. Just become a Freemason, and you may find that no one inside or outside the fraternity will care what you have to say."

Perhaps. But my mind is made up. By the time this book goes on sale, I expect to be a Master Mason. The one person I know that will please is me.

RECOMMENDED READING

Basic Masonry and its philosophy:
The Mystic Tie by Allen E. Roberts, Macoy Publishing Co., P.O. Box 9759, Richmond, VA 23228.

Degrees of Scottish Rite, Southern Jurisdiction:
A Bridge to Light by Dr. Rex R. Hutchens, Supreme Council, Southern Jurisdiction A.A.S.R., 1733 Sixteenth Street N.W., Washington, DC 20009.

Masonic charities:
Masonic Philanthropies: A Tradition of Caring by Dr. S. Brent Morris, Supreme Council A.A.S.R., Southern Jurisdiction, 1733 Sixteenth Street N.W., Washington, DC 20009; Northern Jurisdiction, P.O. Box 519, Lexington, MA 02173.